The Remarriage Adventure provides a wealth of information that will help you avoid common pitfalls as you chart a course for remarriage success. Don't embark on this lifelong journey without a plan, read *The Remarriage Adventure*.

—Peter J. Larson, Ph.D., Co-Author of
PREPARE/ENRICH Life Innovations

Dale and Susan Mathis look at the elements of remarriage in a practical and realistic way, since they are living it themselves. *The Remarriage Adventure* is a great resource that addresses the complexities of remarriage and blending a family.

—Scott and Bethany Palmer, The Money Couple,
Authors of *First Comes Love, Then Comes Money*

D1450415

Praise for
The Remarriage Adventure

The high divorce rate among couples who remarry is about to drop . . . dramatically. *The Remarriage Adventure* is a thorough, intensely practical, biblical, hands-on guide. If you want a successful remarriage—and of course you do—you must get this book. I believe it will make a difference.

—David Clarke, Ph.D., Christian Psychologist,
Speaker, and Author of *Married . . . But Lonely*

In *The Remarriage Adventure,* Dale and Susan Mathis give hope to couples who are blending their families. This book is a roadmap for success, combining spiritual principles and practical strategies to empower couples to succeed in remarriage. A must-read for any couple on this journey!

—Catherine Hammond, Trust Lawyer/Counselor
and Founder of Hammond Law Group, LLC

The Remarriage Adventure is an invaluable resource for couples who are setting out on the journey of remarriage and blending families, as well as for pastors who increasingly require insight into their unique challenges. The power of coupling their own story with those of others enables Dale and Susan to offer biblically practical wisdom from a foundation of compassionate understanding. Highly recommended!

—Grant R. Walton, Senior Pastor, New Creation
Family Church, Johannesburg, South Africa

Journey with Susan and Dale Mathis as they lead you into a new adventure of preparing for remarriage and redemptive love. Written with warmth, wit, biblical encouragement, and practical insight, *The Remarriage Adventure* is a must-read for couples planning to marry again.

—Jackie M. Johnson, Author of *When Love Ends
and the Ice Cream Carton Is Empty*

As in the reality show called *Wipe Out*, the complexity of obstacles like finances, blending children into a new family, in-laws, and healing from past wounds can make the average remarried couple feel like they are one step away from a huge wipe out! Fortunately, Dale and Susan Mathis have written a wonderful resource to help you navigate this obstacle course with biblical principles and practical advice. Most importantly, their emphasis on the redemptive love of Jesus Christ is the signpost that will encourage you through the most difficult of circumstances.

—Dr. Juli Slattery, Author of *No More Headaches*
and *Finding the Hero in your Husband*

If you would like a deeper understanding on how to have a better marriage, *The Remarriage Adventure* is for you! With biblical practicality, sprinkled with situations that are unique to stepfamilies, this resource provides help, hope, and valuable insight for any Christian couple.

—Laura Petherbridge, Speaker and Author
of *When "I Do" Becomes "I Don't"*

In *The Remarriage Adventure: Preparing for a Lifetime of Love and Happiness*, Susan and Dale Mathis share what they and other couples have learned as they've blended their families, providing valuable tips and skills that will help *your* new marriage succeed and thrive.

—Michelle Cox, Author of *Simple Little Words*
and *Mothers Who Made a Difference*

The Remarriage Adventure should be a mandatory read for any couple thinking about or planning to remarry. Susan and Dale's rich biblical guidance will strengthen any couple and prepare them to marry and blend their family.

—Mitch Temple, Author of *The Marriage Turnaround*,
Speaker, Consultant to Christian Organizations and Films

the Re-Marriage Adventure

the

Re-Marriage
Adventure

*Preparing for a lifetime
of love & happiness*

SUSAN & DALE MATHIS

Tyndale House Publishers, Inc.
Carol Stream, Illinois

A Focus on the Family book published by Tyndale House Publishers, Inc., Carol Stream, Illinois 60188

Focus on the Family and the accompanying logo and design are federally registered trademarks of Focus on the Family, Colorado Springs, CO 80995.

TYNDALE and Tyndale's quill logo are registered trademarks of Tyndale House Publishers, Inc.

All Scripture quotations, unless otherwise indicated, are taken from the *Holy Bible, New International Version*®. NIV®. Copyright © 1973, 1978, 1984 by Biblica, Inc.™ Used by permission of Zondervan. All rights reserved worldwide. Scripture quotations marked (KJV) are taken from the *King James Version.*

People's names and certain details of their stories have been changed to protect the privacy of the individuals involved. However, the facts of what happened and the underlying principles have been conveyed as accurately as possible.

The use of material from or references to various Web sites does not imply endorsement of those sites in their entirety.

Editor: Brandy Bruce
Cover Design by Julie Chen
Cover photograph copyright © Irene Suchocki. All rights reserved.

Library of Congress Cataloging-in-Publication Data
Mathis, Susan, 1957-
   The remarriage adventure : preparing for a lifetime of love and happiness / by Susan and Dale Mathis.
      p. cm.
   Includes bibliographical references and index.
   ISBN 978-1-58997-721-1 (alk. paper)
   1. Remarriage—Religious aspects—Christianity. I. Mathis, Dale, 1941- II. Title.
BV838.M38 2012
248.8'44—dc23
                                    2012015564

Printed in the United States of America

1 2 3 4 5 6 7 8 9 /18 17 16 15 14 13 12

We dedicate this book to the amazing second-marriage couples who have become a special part of our lives through sharing their stories with us—and with you. These couples—and many others—are walking out the reality that God's redemptive plan for marriage and family life can be sweeter than any of us anticipated. These couples have marriages that are strong and successful, blending-family journeys that are adventurous, and lives that are testimonies of what God can do in those who seek, serve, and follow Him.

We also dedicate this book to you, our readers, who are so very wise in taking the time to prepare for the adventure of your second marriage. May the journey be life-changing, exciting, and filled with God's love leading and guiding you.

Contents

Acknowledgments

So many people have touched our lives as we've walked together through life's ups and downs. You have imparted your wisdom into our lives so that we can now share God's redemptive plan with those we serve and with our readers.

Thanks to all our friends and family members who have encouraged us during this adventure of writing, have shared your lives and stories with us, have given of yourselves in priceless ways, and have enriched our lives—and now help us enrich the lives of our readers.

Thanks to each of you who has encouraged us along the way and helped us see what God has in store for us. We trust you know who you are and how special you are to us.

Thanks to Larry, Brandy, Allison, and Chris at Focus on the Family, who have worked with us on this project. It's great to have such a supportive team.

Thanks to you, our readers, for allowing God's Word and these pages to speak into your lives. We pray that they will empower you to better prepare for the adventure of remarriage and help you be successful in your blending-family journey.

And most of all, thanks to God for allowing us to be a part of this project. We are humbled to serve You in making Your great redemptive plan known.

Welcome to
the Adventure!

Second marriage, remarriage, stepfamily, blending family, nontra-
ditional family, extended family, secondary family, combined fam-
ily, blended family—who are you really becoming? Whatever you call it,
when you marry for a second time (or more), you are entering into an
unprecedented adventure. It'll be work. It'll be challenging. It may even
feel impossible at times. But it's one of the most amazing opportunities to
experience the beauty of redemption!

Since almost three out of four remarriages fail, you're wise in taking the
time to prepare for your second marriage, and we're delighted to journey
with you through this experience. Susan and I (Dale) both experienced the
heartache of previous failed marriages, as well as the challenges of growing
up in homes where each of our fathers was deceased. So our heart's desire is
to help you get ready for your marriage and keep you from going through
any more of the trauma, grief, and pain you've already experienced.

Statistics say that couples who participate in premarital education report a 30 percent higher level of overall marital satisfaction and better

communication.[1] That means you're greatly increasing your chances for success by reading this book and preparing for the adventure of a second marriage!

Your past marriage, whether it ended through death or divorce, will affect your second marriage to some degree. Perhaps one or both of you have children still at home. Maybe one of you has never been married or has never had children, and the other is a widow or widower with kids. Maybe you both come from a divorce situation, and your kids are still stinging from its pain. Perhaps one or both of you have full custody, or one or both of you have part-time custody and have to juggle crazy schedules of kids coming in and out of the home at different times. Or you may be in an even more complex situation! Even if you're empty nesters, adult kids will likely still affect your second marriage.

I (Susan) had a bit of most of these scenarios in my history. My dad died three months before I was born, so for four years my widowed mother was a single parent. Then she married my stepdad, who always made sure I stayed in my stepchild role, saying, "You don't count; you're a stepkid."

I grew up with three half siblings, but when I was eighteen I found out I had three more half siblings from my dad's first marriage! Talk about confusing. Dale and I have five children between us, and although this means each of us has stepchildren, we don't consider them that. Yes, it's complicated, but much of it depends on how you view it all.

For most second-marriage couples, one or both partners are likely bringing children into the marriage. That makes you what is often called a blending family (or one of the many other labels mentioned earlier), and because it's such a complex situation, premarital preparation is all the more important. Dale and I are keenly aware that one of the reasons for our failed marriages is that we didn't have a manual like this to help us prepare for and understand the complexities of marriage. We pray that this book will bring you the insight, help, and hope you need.

Not only is remarriage often very complicated, especially when children are involved, but it is also a huge commitment, so it shouldn't be taken lightly. And because you're a second-marriage couple, there's so much more to think about besides the wedding. It's all the other stuff that matters so much—the for better *or worse*, for richer *or poorer*, *in sickness* or in health, till *death* do us part, the daily-living-together and blending-a-family stuff. Knowing how to work through the challenges of a second marriage and the intricacies of blending a family—before you get into the heat of it—will help you be more successful than you could ever be without this information.

We want to encourage you with this book and make sure you know that even though you'll probably experience some challenges ahead, especially during the first few years, your marriage can also be one of the most healing, exciting, and wonderful experiences of your life! Dale and I have found this to be true in our own marriage.

This book will help you experience these things as well. Some of it will review basics, such as what commitment, love, and marriage are all about, while most of it will go much deeper and may address things you've never thought you needed to talk about. If you see this premarital preparation as an adventure, a journey deeper into the life of the one you love and into creating a blending family that will stand the test of time, it'll be one of the most important things you can do.

Throughout this book, we'll share stories from other second-marriage couples who have experienced the struggles and successes of remarriage as well as blending a family. We know that you'll make some of your own mistakes along the way, just as they and we have done. But their stories will assure you that the Lord will faithfully walk you through it all as you trust in Him.

We hope to help each of you better understand yourself, your future spouse, and your future life together as a couple and as a blending family; to help alleviate your fears, doubts, and worries about yourself, your future mate, and your marriage; to help you prepare for living together and loving each other forever; and to launch you on a joyful journey of marital adventure and a lifetime of growing together.

We'll also ask you to review your past to better understand how your previous marriages, families, and experiences have molded your lives. You'll try to articulate your expectations, beliefs, attitudes, concerns, fears, and struggles, and even assess how ready you are to remarry at this time. And you'll glean helpful ideas on how to handle issues you'll face from the couples who share their stories about how they worked through second-marriage issues, including communication, roles, in-law challenges, sexuality, finances, and conflict resolution.

Though we'll address some of the blending-family issues you may encounter, the primary purpose of this book is to help you prepare for your second marriage. So we'll concentrate on the two of you getting to know each other better—more than you ever dreamed possible. After all, your marriage will be the foundation of your family, and your family can only be as strong and healthy as your relationship as a couple!

Be careful not to enter your second marriage hoping to change your future mate, or you'll likely be disappointed. Lifetime habits don't usually change, and people are who they are. We strongly suggest you walk into this preparation time with the view that you want to know each other better, to learn how compatible you are, and to find out ways to make your second marriage a success.

To be effective, it's essential that you choose, right now, to be open, honest, and even vulnerable with each other. If you try to hide anything, we can almost guarantee it'll come up after you marry, and it might be hurtful to your spouse, your relationship, and your blending family. So get it all out in the open now. If you do, you'll build trust, understanding, and intimacy. We know that you realize that neither of you is perfect, so be sure you know each other deep inside—your strengths and weaknesses—even those things you may have wanted to hide.

As you work through the pages of this book, we want to encourage you to go through it with others—a pastor, a counselor, a mature couple, or a small group. These people can walk you through areas that are hard to talk through or issues that are confusing, scary, or just tough. They can provide you with another perspective when you need it, and they can keep you accountable.

In fact, before you begin, we strongly encourage you to meet with your pastor or a Christian counselor to discuss what the Bible has to say about remarriage, as well as talk through your individual feelings and beliefs regarding remarriage. Depending on your specific situation, there may be significant biblical and/or spiritual issues that need to be addressed before moving forward. Also, you may have been raised to have different perspectives on this important topic, so discussing your feelings and making sure that remarriage is the right path for you is a healthy place to start.

We also suggest you work through this book at your own pace and try not to skip topics you think you already understand. You may find you need to slow down when you hit speed bumps where the two of you disagree or when you find it difficult to work through a topic.

And don't give up! Persevere together and glean everything you can out of each chapter. If you find you need more help in a certain area, check out the list of resources at the end of the book. Be a lifelong learner, especially about the topics of marriage and blending a family. Every resource you work through can help you on your journey.

As a companion to this book, we strongly encourage you to assess your relationship by taking the PREPARE/ENRICH (Premarital Counseling and Marriage Enrichment) used by professional counselors, pastors, trained and certified mentors, and churches that conduct premarital courses. (Go to www.prepare-enrich.com for more information.)

We have used this assessment with numerous couples and find it to be considerably accurate and reliable. Once you've taken the PREPARE/ENRICH, counselors are able to help you assess your potential for marital success as well as understand the areas of strength and weakness within your relationship. Then you can discuss issues that might be difficult or overlooked. The objective is to encourage and inform you, not discourage you.

By reading this book and taking the PREPARE/ENRICH, you'll enter into your second marriage with wisdom, understanding, and lots of tools to help you be successful along the way. Your expectations will be more realistic, and you'll be more committed to your marriage. That's good assurance . . . and insurance.

Finally, please know that we've changed many of the names in our stories to protect people's privacy, but the examples represent real-life situations couples face. Let's join these couples and learn from their journeys. Welcome to the adventure of remarriage!

Redemption Is Real

What Is God's View of Love and Remarriage?

*M*aggie had waited nearly three years to remarry. Her divorce had been traumatic, and her two children felt abandoned by their dad and were still angry. *A new daddy will help,* Maggie thought. *Our loneliness might finally go away.* When Maggie met Sam, she felt he was the ticket out of her difficult life. Soon they were planning to get married.

But as the wedding drew near, Maggie and Sam began to argue about the wedding details and a lot more, and the children began to act out. Maggie's deep feelings of anger, bitterness, and resentment from her past resurfaced when Sam started to disagree with anything she suggested, large or small.

Sam realized that there must be bigger issues, so he wisely suggested they get some counseling. Maggie reluctantly agreed. At the first premarital counseling session, the suggestion to postpone the wedding was met with Maggie's stiff opposition. But when Sam insisted, Maggie started down a road of healing she didn't even know she needed.

The Grieving Process

For the next eight months, Maggie walked through the stages of grief, which led to healing and hope. She had stuffed away so much pain, frustration, confusion, and bitterness. Yes, she'd experienced the stages of shock, denial, and anger; she had even attempted to bargain with God as she went through the divorce itself. But even after the divorce process ended, the anger stayed, and with it, depression. She thought that the only way out was to find someone new who could deliver her from all the hurt she'd experienced.

Though Sam had brought a measure of happiness and hope into her life, Maggie had pushed back the memories, anger, and bitterness of her first marriage until she could no longer hold those things in. Her short temper and the sarcastic comments that surfaced while she and Sam were planning the wedding were just symptoms of a bigger problem.

As she worked through the stages of forgiveness toward her ex and acceptance of the loss of her first marriage, peace and hope led to joy that she didn't think she could ever have. She was finally beginning to resolve the heartache she thought would be a part of her life forever.

As Sam patiently walked through all this with Maggie, he dealt with some issues of his own. Sam still harbored unresolved bitterness toward God because of his wife's sudden and unexpected death. Once he realized this about himself, he no longer had to work so hard to hold his tongue and keep his emotions in check. He acknowledged his hurt and eventually found peace with God. He, too, realized that the pain of losing his wife needed to be resolved before he and Maggie entered this new marriage.

Both Maggie and Sam were so glad they took the time to work through their issues before they entered their new life together. They also realized that this delay in getting married gave their children time to heal and resolve their own issues. The kids received counseling, and Maggie, Sam, and the children attended family counseling sessions together.

Finally Maggie, Sam, and the children were ready to unite as a family.

A year after Maggie and Sam had postponed their wedding the first time, they were on their way to becoming a healthy blending family.

Redemption

Whether you've lost your marriage through a death or a divorce, pain is a natural part of any loss, and redemption is God's plan for healing that pain. As a couple, having a vision for a redemptive marriage can be one of the most inspiring, productive, and motivating ways to view your future together.

Scripture says, "Where there is no vision, the people perish" (Proverbs 29:18, KJV). Having a "vision" means having a plan to do life together God's way. That vision will help you overcome the challenges life might bring. A vision for a redemptive second marriage will guide you and help you grow through the stresses of blending a family. When you have a positive and exciting vision for doing life together, you can work together productively, even when times are tough.

What did this look like for us? Dale and I (Susan) agreed that our vision was to live the message of Jesus Christ's redeeming love through our relationship. By caring for each other physically, emotionally, spiritually, and every other way, we wanted to create a fully intimate and inspiring relationship that could show our children and grandchildren, family, and friends the beauty and promise of God's plan for marriage.

What do we mean by *redemption*? According to Webster's online dictionary, to *redeem* is "to buy or get back, to pay off, to ransom, to deliver, to restore, or to make amends for." Wow! As your Redeemer, God can buy back your past and deliver you from your broken dreams, your heartaches, your mistakes and sins, your fears, and your pain. He can restore your joy and hope, and so much more. He knows that none of us are perfect, and He forgives so we can forgive ourselves and others. He can heal, deliver, and transform you into healthy, holy individuals if you allow Him to work in your lives and in your marriage relationship.

A redemptive marriage is more powerful than either of you—or even both of you put together. It's God's plan to make you, as a couple, all He intends you to be. In an atmosphere of accountability, safety, and grace, we can create a place where we leave our selfish tendencies behind and become more like Jesus.

While we were dating, Dale and I (Susan) drove to Estes Park, Colorado, to get away and visit some friends. We sat overlooking the beautiful mountains, sharing our past pain and heartache and asking each other question after question. It was a great place to discuss the possibility of our future together, to explore whether we were ready for a redemptive marriage. We promised to reveal our thoughts, fears, goals, and needs to each other completely before even considering a second marriage.

Every night for several weeks after our time in the mountains, we made lists of things we wanted to know about each other—everything from how we were raised to finances, roles and goals, expectations and pet peeves, sex and health issues, our previous marriages and children, our relationships with God, and so much more. Each question prompted twenty more, and some of the questions were serious, deep, and scary.

Dale and I had both been single for more than a decade. We'd been deeply hurt by our earlier failed relationships, and we worried we might not be able to be successful in the future. Although we had tried to learn all we could about love, relationships, and God's vision for a redemptive remarriage, being open and honest made us feel very vulnerable. We realized this kind of openness could make or break our budding relationship. But we also decided that without complete honesty, we'd be marrying a person we didn't really know. And although we were in love and wanted to move forward in our relationship, we first needed to know God's plan for us.

What Is Redeeming Love?

How can we define love, a redeeming love that is life-changing? Though there are many definitions of *love*, the Bible gives the best definition in the

Love Chapter, 1 Corinthians 13:4–8. You've probably memorized it, but let's review it here:

> Love is patient, love is kind. It does not envy, it does not boast, it is
> not proud. It is not rude, it is not self-seeking, it is not easily angered,
> it keeps no record of wrongs. Love does not delight in evil but rejoices
> with the truth. It always protects, always trusts, always hopes, always
> perseveres. Love never fails.

Having tasted the pain of love lost, none of us want to experience that kind of pain again. These few verses give us a framework for how to love in a redemptive way—in a way that will buy or get back, pay off, ransom, deliver, restore, or make amends for the brokenness, guilt, sorrow, pain, hurts, and losses of life.

Yet although we may strive for this ideal, we won't always love perfectly, and besides, redemption is a lifetime journey. Sometimes we'll simply fall short. But as long as we're pressing on to love as much as we're able, we are showing redeeming love. If we understand this, we'll give each other space to make mistakes and then grace to move on. This book will help you learn how to do this well.

Throughout this book we'll unpack 1 Corinthians 13 and learn how to better love in the redeeming way God intends us to love each other. We'll offer practical and helpful ways to put God's love into practice. Growing into a loving person is a gradual process that begins by imitating the character of Christ.

What's Covenant Commitment?

Dale and I (Susan) believe strongly in the power of redemption and the ongoing work that redeeming love has in our lives. We also know that we can't love like that without God's help and an unwavering commitment to the covenant we made on our wedding day.

In our living room is a symbol we used in our wedding. It's a three-fold cord of red, white, and gold strands. For us, it symbolizes that the commitment we made to marriage wasn't just between the two of us; it was a covenant between three of us, with God at the center. The Bible tells us, "A cord of three strands is not quickly broken" (Ecclesiastes 4:12). That's how Dale and I want our commitment to be—strong, steady, God-centered, able to withstand life's storms.

Of all the major decisions we make in life, making a commitment to get married, especially a second (or maybe even a third) time, is one of the most important—and often the hardest. Yet too many people spend less time and energy choosing a lifetime partner than they do researching a potential home or car! Unfortunately, many also think they can trade in their spouse, like a used car, if things don't work out. Because you're reading this book, it's obvious that you're not like most people, and we honor you both for being wise enough to take the time and energy to prepare for the adventure of a second marriage.

Another problem in our society today is cohabitation, even among Christian couples. Many of the couples who have come to us for counseling have lived together already. They profess to be Christians, but their lifestyle doesn't support that claim. Many don't see a problem with living together. They want to be sure they are "compatible" before they commit, especially a second time. For many of those couples who kept cohabitating and eventually did marry, the trust and intimacy they sacrificed by living together affected their marriage.

Cohabitation—or even sex before marriage—is problematic because it's false intimacy. (We'll discuss this topic further in chapter 9.) It distorts your view of the other person and hinders the development of a deep, emotional, trusting, and intimate relationship necessary for a successful lifetime of marriage. It also changes the dynamic of the relationship and sets a poor example for your children. And for those individuals who are Christians, cohabitating and having premarital sex are counter to God's plan for relationships. Scriptures such as Hebrews 13:4 give strong instruction to keep sex within the confines of marriage.

If you're already living together like many of the couples we've counseled, take a moment to talk about the ramifications of your decision. Decide now to abstain from sex until your wedding night. Brainstorm some ideas on how you could feasibly live apart until your wedding. Could one of you move in with relatives or a close friend? Though it's not convenient, couples who make this sacrifice never regret it. It will not only benefit your relationship, but it will also show your children that you're serious about starting your marriage out right.

As you know, a trouble-free warranty doesn't come with your marriage certificate. Most couples know that a second marriage is hard work, and there will be lots of speed bumps in the road, especially when they're blending a family.

A covenant commitment to your marriage is a promise to keep your relationship vibrant and alive, even when the feelings aren't that strong. Covenant promises are unconditional—there are no escape clauses or money-back guarantees. They are made on the foundation of faith and love, and they are permanent.

Even if you've lost the permanence of your first marriage, God's redemptive plan is available to you. God has promised that He can make all things new; He's given you a definition of love, a blueprint for covenant commitment, and His grace-filled plan for marriage through His Word. But for all this to work, you have to rely on His wisdom, strength, and guidance along the way.

If you feel distant from God at the moment, choose now to reconnect and make Him the center of your life and marriage. This might mean finding a church that will work for both of you and that has children's or youth programs that fit your family well. Or it might mean that you start praying and reading the Bible together or join a couple's Bible study. Whatever it takes, make God the center of your new life together.

God loved us so much that He planned for us to know the joy of a lifetime through a committed relationship in all its aspects. The problem is, commitment often rubs against our selfish interests because it requires that we set aside those interests and care for another person more than for ourselves. Susan and I (Dale) have to continually recalibrate, refocus, and reengage when one of us gets a little selfish or sideways. It's not easy, but it's doable.

It's all about choice, and some choices are hard. But just as God gave us the choice to love Him, so we have the choice to love each other on a moment-by-moment basis. Covenant commitment isn't based just on a romantic feeling; it's a choice to be faithful physically, emotionally, mentally, and spiritually, day by day.

A covenant commitment provides a stark alternative to the temporary, fly-by-night relationships the world offers—the ones often presented by Hollywood and the media. This kind of commitment visibly shows God's plan for a godly marriage, no matter how imperfect we may be, and it gives us a safe place to love and grow together.

What's a Redemptive Marriage?

Marriage is the legal, social, and spiritual contract between a man and woman. A redemptive marriage is also God's way of showing His love for us, showing His plan to the world, and helping us become more like Him.

Shortly after Susan and I (Dale) were engaged, I was diagnosed with prostate cancer. I was shocked because I've been so healthy all my life. The word *cancer* is extra-frightening to me because my older brother died of kidney cancer at age seventeen. Conflicting emotions made my heart pound—the fear of dying much sooner than expected was suddenly very real to me.

Then, what about Susan? I wondered how I would tell her and how she would react. What if the cancer spread and our journey together ended much sooner than we had anticipated? Where's the redemption in that? How could this happen now, just when we were planning our future together? I knew I could be facing the toughest battle of my life.

First I had to tell Susan and give her the opportunity to back out of the engagement. I knew this promise we were about to make—to love and serve each other through sickness and health—shouldn't have to be tested until long after we were married. At least that's what I thought.

I told her everything. I explained to her the treatment options—none of which were appealing—and then I had to tell her there was a more than 50 percent chance of impotency. I'm sure she was terrified, but she had already made the decision to marry me—for the rest of her life, even if cancer took one of us much earlier than we ever would have dreamed.

We cried and prayed for courage and wisdom to make the right choices, and for healing and a long life together. We did our homework, got four doctors' opinions, and proceeded with the treatment. This filled our first year of marriage with a multitude of challenges, concerns, fears, and worries.

What got us through this difficult time was knowing that God had a plan, a redemptive plan, for our lives together. As it turned out, this book and our first book were inspired by the knowledge that we're here for such a brief time, and during that time, God wants us to make a difference in other people's lives, just as He's made in ours. We laugh about it today, especially when one of our friends quipped that Susan should have had me inspected before we got engaged. Yet today we're thankful that the cancer is in remission, and our marriage is stronger because of the trial we faced together.

When a couple marries, God takes two unique people and unites their souls and bodies for a common purpose for the rest of their lives. But He also takes two imperfect people and puts them in a committed relationship so they can safely grow and be transformed together as they work on their imperfections and problems.

When people see imperfect marriages or experience marriages that fail, they sometimes think that marriage must have been a mistake. But God's perfect plan for marriage isn't flawed; it's people who make it less than God designed. Fortunately, marriage is a special place where God can work on our flaws—hopefully in a safe and loving environment.

Marriage is for living out God's redemptive plan and becoming more like Him every day. It's seeing your mate grow through the love, grace, and forgiveness you freely give him or her, while that person also allows you to grow, even through your mistakes. It's about giving, helping, serving, trusting, forgiving, caring, learning, and living through the ups and downs of life. It's applying 1 Corinthians 13 and watching God work through that process.

A Deeper Kind of Love

The Bible also explains that God's perfect plan remains the same—He wants us to rise above the cultural norms and be transformed by the wonderful adventure of married life. We can see this through all the scriptures that validate His plan, such as Matthew 19:4–6 and Ephesians 5:22–33.

But that's not as easy as it sounds. In today's culture, marriage is often viewed simply as a way to make us happy. Couples think they can create their own rules and way of life—whatever suits their personal desires. But this kind of selfish love will result in a poor marriage, especially when a couple is trying to blend a family. By its very nature, marriage requires teamwork, sharing, sacrifice, and growing together every day. It requires making daily choices about large and small things and choosing to consider each other's feelings and needs for the good of the relationship.

In a marriage relationship, you must consistently choose your relationship over material things, over other people, over work, over other desires, including your children's desires—sometimes even over ministry or other noble deeds.

One of our friends nearly lost her marriage because she was so busy working at her church that she neglected her relationship with her husband. You have to choose your relationship with your spouse over other pursuits, even if it sometimes means choosing to forgo something you wanted or setting aside your feelings for the sake of your spouse.

As you read this, you might be feeling a little overwhelmed. Most couples feel that way at one time or another. But we want to encourage you that being determined to start out right is so much better than falling into patterns that will ultimately be detrimental to your relationship. Going through this book together gives you an opportunity to talk about what you both want your second marriage to look like. By talking about these things, you can then be intentional about changing what you need to change. Your marriage will be much stronger if you do.

Marriage is so much about working on your character, being the right person, and changing as you and your spouse grow and mature together. None of us are perfect, and understanding this up front is important. We are all works in progress. As you strive to grow and become more like Christ, and your future spouse is working to become more Christlike too, your relationship will deepen and grow stronger.

Marriage can give you purpose, meaning, a redeeming love that knows no bounds, and a commitment that brings security and happiness beyond your wildest dreams. It also helps shape you into the person of character that God intends you to be. In living out your commitment to love and serve each other unconditionally in marriage, you model the kind of redeeming love that can show the world, and your kids, a better way.

Congratulations! You're on your way to becoming ready for the greatest adventure of life—a redemptive remarriage!

❧ BLENDING WITH KIDS

Helping Your Children Understand God's View of Forgiveness and Remarriage

Just like you, children can experience the beauty of redemption. As they see God work in your lives, walk through the process of grieving, and move into a place of healthy living, they will learn that you serve a big God who heals and transforms lives.

Still, it's crucial that you keep in mind that death or divorce hurts children deeply, and because they have neither the maturity nor the tools to work through their pain, confusion, and emotions, it's *your* job to walk them through it. There may be times when a counselor or a wise third party can help them even better than you can.

Children can easily blame themselves for a divorce or even the death of a parent. They can be angry with you and/or God. They often have a lot of rational and irrational emotions, thoughts, and concerns that need to be dealt with. And they can learn to view marriage as flawed rather than the people involved in it.

If your child still suffers from the loss of his or her biological family or seems unsure about the possibility of your remarrying, find a trustworthy counselor, pastor, or wise friend to work with your child. Your child also needs to walk through the grieving process to be ready for the adventure of your remarriage.

We urge you to read *The Smart Stepfamily* by Ron Deal, as well as other stepfamily/blended-family resources. (See the recommended reading list at the back of the book.) Though we'll touch on these issues in the following chapters, reading specific stepfamily/blended-family books can help you with the intricacies of blending a family much more thoroughly. Just as you need to prepare for the adventure of remarriage, you also need to prepare for the adventure of blending your family.

Let's Define a Few Words

Because remarriage and blending a family can be so complicated, here are a few definitions of words we'll be using throughout the book:

- *Remarriage*—A marriage where at least one individual has been previously married one or more times. One individual may have never been married, or both may have previously been married. The previous marriage(s) may have ended in a death or a divorce. For the purposes of simplicity, we'll refer to "remarriage" or "second marriage."

- *Blending family* (also called a blended family or stepfamily)—A family that includes at least one child from a previous marriage, a biological parent, and a stepparent.
- *Biological parent*—A parent who is connected to a child by birth, whether in the home or not.
- *Stepparent*—A parent who is not connected to a child by birth but is connected by marriage to the child's mother or father.
- *Stepchild*—A child who is not connected to the parent by birth but is connected by marriage to the child's mother or father.

⚘ APPRAISING MY LIFE

Looking back on what you've learned about redemption, write your own definition of *redemptive marriage.*

⚘ ASSESSING OUR LIVES

What's your vision for remarriage? Read Psalm 127:1, Proverbs 24: 3–4, and Matthew 7:24–27. A vision is having common goals that are bigger than your everyday circumstances and feelings. Create a plan together and be strategic about carrying it out. Be specific about your time frame and how you will achieve your goals. For example, what are your marriage goals? What about goals regarding your children? What about your individual life goals and dreams?

List five things you want to include in the vision for your marriage:

1.

2.

3.

4.

5.

Share with each other what your vision for your second marriage entails. What does it look like to you? How will you fulfill it? Each of your ideas may be different. That's okay. You'll need to work together to find a united vision in the midst of those differences. If you can't resolve your differences, be sure to consult someone who can help you work through them now. As you develop and refine a clear vision for your marriage, the exciting vision of the marriage God has for you will be evident. Revisit your vision statement often. Establish one-, two-, and five-year goals, as well as a lifetime vision.

☘ A MOMENT FOR FUN!

What advice would you have given Adam and Eve?

Imagine being infamous for one thing. What would it be?

☘ APPLYING GOD'S WORD

God established specific reasons to marry. Like the concept of the Trinity—
Father, Son, and Holy Spirit are separate but one—you and your future
spouse become one in marriage. You communicate, create, serve, give,
sacrifice, relate to each other, and can lead others to Him. Read the following
scriptures together and answer three or more of the questions as you reflect
on the previous information you've read.

Why Are You Created in God's Image?

Then God said, "Let us make man in our image, in our likeness, and
let them rule over the fish of the sea and the birds of the air, over the
livestock, over all the earth, and over all the creatures that move along
the ground." So God created man in his own image, in the image
of God he created him; male and female he created them. (Genesis
1:26–27)

What Are God's Priorities about Love?

"Love the Lord your God with all your heart and with all your soul
and with all your mind." This is the first and greatest commandment.
And the second is like it: "Love your neighbor as yourself." (Matthew
22:37–39)

How Should You Love Each Other?

You, my brothers, were called to be free. But do not use your freedom to indulge the sinful nature; rather, serve one another in love. (Galatians 5:13)

As a Couple, What Is Your Ultimate Purpose on Earth?

A new command I [Jesus] give you: Love one another. As I have loved you, so you must love one another. By this all men will know that you are my disciples, if you love one another. (John 13:34–35)

What Is God's Vision for Your Marriage?

Ephesians 5:22–33. (You can read this in your Bible.)

Ready or Not

Are You Ready for Remarriage?

When asked why they wanted to marry, Anne and Pete quickly responded that they loved each other. But as with most of the couples we've counseled over the years, digging a little deeper revealed much more complex reasons.

After Anne and Pete analyzed their motives and their hearts, Anne realized that deep down she needed financial help, and she longed for a father for her son. Pete discovered he desperately wanted to end the loneliness that gnawed at his heart, and he needed help with his three kids. Anne wanted to replace all those bad memories from her failed marriage with new, good ones. Pete thought he could leave his past behind and start his life over. And while each of these were valid needs and goals, Anne and Pete began to understand how these reasons for marrying might affect their future together—for good or for bad.

By digging deeper into their motivations, Anne and Pete also realized that they needed to prepare for their second marriage by equipping themselves with wisdom and understanding about their relationship, as well as learning how to blend a family. And they needed the tools that would help them through the challenges that would likely come. Once they adequately prepared, Anne and Pete were much better equipped to remarry.

Knowing Why

Do you know why you want to be remarried? God wants your second marriage to be redemptive, successful, and fulfilling. But before you move forward, you need to do your part to make sure you're ready for the adventure of remarriage at this juncture in your life.

Thankfully, Susan and I (Dale) each took our time to figure this out before we even met each other. I was single for almost two decades and got my first master's degree in marriage and family counseling partially to figure out what went wrong in my first marriage. Until I met Susan, I just wasn't sure I ever wanted to remarry.

Susan spent more than ten years reading relationship books, going to counseling, and working hard to figure out what went wrong in her previous marriage. Through it all, she realized how her dysfunctional childhood and first marriage affected the way she thought about marriage and related to others. She started dating and then realized she had more "stuff" to deal with. So she stopped dating to work on her issues and then tried dating again. By the time we met, she'd dealt with those emotional issues that affected her outlook on marriage.

Looking back, we both can honestly say that assessing ourselves and our potential mates was a very wise thing to do. Although you can't possibly solve every problem, and neither of you will ever be perfect, you can work through your issues and move forward with the attitude of continually becoming better people.

Although it's often difficult to fully understand and articulate the underlying reasons you want to marry, we believe it's essential for you to take the time to think this through. Like Anne and Pete, there may be multiple reasons, and that's okay. Just be honest and explore your needs, desires, and motivations so you know what you're working with. This chapter will help you do just that.

But before you analyze all this, ask God for wisdom and discernment and resolve to be patient and caring with each other. Your goal is to learn about and understand your future mate's heart, to grow closer together, and to be sure you're both ready for the adventure of remarriage. You want to thoroughly count all the costs involved in making a commitment to remarry and blend a family.

Your first step is to look inward, to do a little self-analysis. Ask for help from a trusted friend, a respected family member, or perhaps a professional.

Take a few minutes to finish the following statements:

1. I love him/her because . . . (Name at least five reasons why you love this person.)
2. I want to marry him/her because . . . (Name five reasons why you want to marry this person.)
3. I believe we are a good match because . . . (Name five reasons why you think you are compatible.)

In addition, now is a good time to assess why you may want to marry at this point in your life. Remember, there are no right or wrong answers; it's your honest evaluation that's important.

You may feel that remarriage will make your life easier and help you through difficult times. And sometimes it does. But more often than not, the first few years of remarriage will be challenging, especially if you're blending a family with children in the home.

Please know that this chapter was written not to discourage you from remarrying but to help you as you prepare. Evaluating these things will greatly increase your chances for success in building a solid marriage and a healthy blending family.

Through this assessment, you may realize that you are rebounding from a broken relationship or a divorce. Or maybe, like Anne, you realize you want help with your kids or a replacement parent for your children. Could it be that all your friends are married, and you feel like the odd one out?

Maybe, like Pete, you think marriage will end your loneliness. Or perhaps you think remarrying will make you feel whole and make your life more meaningful. Maybe you feel guilty about having premarital sex and think marriage will relieve your guilt. Or possibly, like Dale and me (Susan), you may realize that you've found a life companion—someone who can walk through this life with you and help you become all God wants you to be.

You may want to marry so you can meet each other's needs. That's honorable—if you know precisely what those needs are. Another reason may be to find true intimacy, and that's an admirable goal. One of the greatest joys of life is found in sharing yourself with another, and it's truly rewarding when you're married. Susan and I (Dale) find this to be the case, and it's great.

You will also want to take some time to evaluate what you've learned from your previous marriage. What did you do right? What did you do wrong? And if your prior marriage ended in a divorce, what part did you play in its destruction? Knowing this will help you avoid repeating the mistakes of the past.

Once you've assessed your own life, it's important to go back through your list and try to determine why *your partner* may want to marry you. This may be more difficult, but it will help you gain a better understanding of whom you are choosing to spend the rest of your life with—and why.

What's Important?

Each of us has good and not-so-good personality traits that affect our relationships. A servant's heart is one trait that will tell you much about another person, especially your future spouse. The lack of a servant's attitude can be a real danger sign. If your partner is overly self-centered or inconsiderate of you and others—or always wants things his or her way—watch out! And be extra aware if you have children. They need to see and experience selfless love. The truth is, blending a family will require boatloads of selfless love from all of you.

It takes two people serving each other to make a healthy marriage. While they are dating, people tend to put their best foot forward, often masking their inner selves and hiding their true hearts. So it's important to look past the outward facade and discover who that person really is deep down. That's where discernment and perseverance come in.

Again, we recognize that none of us are perfect; we're just trying to do our best—to love well, to work well, to be successful at what we do. What you want to assess is whether your future mate has a habitual pattern of negative, selfish, or self-centered behavior—or if these behaviors are an exception, not the norm. If some negative patterns are present, their regularity and seriousness should be evaluated carefully, and then they need to be weighed against the positive attributes.

Because you may already be deep into this relationship, we realize it may be difficult to be objective. But do what you must to assess and analyze your partner's traits well before you commit to living with him or her for the rest of your life. You may conclude that your future mate has minor imperfections, and the exceptions are okay, or you may realize that something is a deal breaker.

I (Susan) was afraid that if I ever fell for someone, I would likely lose my perspective and discernment and not be able to evaluate that person well. So I had Dale "interrogated" by several of my friends . . . okay, thirty-four of my friends! Though thirty-four opinions was a little overkill, their insight was discerning and wise, helping me not only to see why I was so interested in this man but also to feel free to set aside my fears and concerns about making a lifetime commitment to Dale.

Proceed with Caution

Sometimes you may love a person who isn't spiritually or emotionally healthy and not even realize it. If your future spouse isn't a Christian, hasn't healed from his or her past, is emotionally unstable, or isn't trustworthy, you should stop, take a careful look at the danger signs, and realize how they might affect your life.

Remember Anne? She lived many years in an abusive first marriage because she didn't heed the warning signs. Anne knew her first husband cheated and "fibbed" a bit, but she believed he would change as he matured, as many people do. But Anne refused to see his habitual self-centeredness and dishonesty as warning signs.

Then, after they married, Anne thought that loving her husband meant she could never question him, that she had to forgive everything, and that she had to press on—no matter what. But despite how hard she tried, her first marriage ended when her husband went to live with another woman.

Anne didn't understand that being patient, forgiving, and trusting toward the one you love doesn't mean turning a blind eye to a lack of character. It also doesn't mean you need to put up with immature, self-centered, or angry behavior, especially if it's a regular pattern.

Most of us know when something is wrong. So take the time to discern and pay attention to the danger signs. If you detect any warning signs in the actions, attitudes, or words of your future mate, you should deal with those before you marry. If you don't, like Anne, you will certainly deal with them afterward. Many of these negative behavior patterns won't change, and you'll likely be living with them all your life.

Red Flags

As you can see, this book requires you to ask yourself and your partner a lot of tough questions. That's why we believe it's absolutely essential to be honest with each other.

After years of counseling with and mentoring couples of all ages and backgrounds, Dale and I (Susan) have identified twelve "red flags" that should alert you to possible danger in your relationship. If any of these red flags are present in your life or the life of your future mate, it may be dangerous to move ahead before you resolve them.

1. On the rebound. If you or your future spouse has been single for less than two years or hasn't intentionally worked through the loss of a previous marriage, this is a red flag. Time can't heal all wounds, but it does heal many. If you hop from one relationship to the next without taking time to heal and resolve your past, you'll surely take that pain into your future. Like Maggie and Sam from chapter 1, take the time you need now.

2. Emotional instability. Divorce or death can wreak havoc on a person's emotions and self-esteem. Unless both of you have gone through the stages of grief and are emotionally healthy, you'll likely encounter major challenges in your relationship, now or later. And like Anne and Pete, you need to be emotionally ready to marry, and for the right reasons. Have both of you stabilized emotionally and found peace with your past? If not, one or both of you may need to work through the grieving process.

3. Codependence. You've been through a lot, your children have been through a lot, and so has your future mate. Moving from married to single can be awkward, and sometimes a person never finds contentment in his or her singleness or individuality. This can lead to becoming codependent on others. Are you independent and comfortable being a single adult, or are you counting on marriage to solve your issues of loneliness, fear, shame, or other challenges? Do you have a healthy relationship with your children, or are you overly dependent on them for your self-esteem or value? It's important to find these things in Christ alone.

4. Addiction. One of the biggest danger signs in a relationship is an addiction to drugs, alcohol, pornography, or gambling, just to name a few. If any of these are present in your relationship, *stop!* Don't deny that an addiction will become a problem for your marriage. It will! People with addictions are either running to or from something. If you or your future spouse is struggling with an addiction, you need professional help to resolve it before you marry. We don't recommend trying to solve the problem on your own. Ask for help.

5. *Abuse.* Whether verbal, sexual, physical, or emotional, is there abuse in either of your backgrounds or with your children? Discuss this completely, and if needed, seek professional counsel to ensure that any problems with abuse are thoroughly resolved before you marry. If left un-resolved, abuse and its demons will crop up sooner or later. Better to deal with it now.

6. *Sex before marriage.* Once a couple becomes sexually active, the relationship takes on a distorted dynamic, and it's difficult for real intimacy to develop. Priorities, motivations, and your perspective toward your partner will be different, and long-term trust issues may eventually haunt one or both of you. You may feel obligated to marry out of a sense of guilt. All this makes it nearly impossible to make wise decisions, especially one as important as marriage. But if you've failed in this area, all is not lost. Ask God for forgiveness, ask forgiveness of each other, and choose to remain chaste until your wedding night. Repentance like this reaps great rewards.

7. *Financial irresponsibility.* Many divorces are due to the stress of financial problems, but financial mismanagement is easy to spot. If he's constantly trying to impress you by spending more than he has, or if she's buying the latest fashions even though she can't afford them, your future spouse may be financially irresponsible. How does he or she deal with finances when it comes to the children? Financial irresponsibility is a danger sign you should never ignore. God asks us to be good stewards of our resources, including our money, and we should. (We'll talk about this more in chapter 8.)

8. *A lack of faith.* Before getting married to an unbeliever, stop and consider what you're doing. The Bible says, "Do not be yoked together [or

unequally yoked] with unbelievers" (2 Corinthians 6:14). If one of you is a Christian but the other is not or is from another faith, this is in conflict with God's plan for you. Having major differences in your spiritual beliefs isn't a small matter, especially when children are involved, and a lack of spiritual leadership in the home will only bring frustration and conflict. Make sure you are equally yoked spiritually before you give your life to each other. This is God's mandate, and you are wise to abide by it.

9. A critical nature. Is your partner critical of you or people in general? The wounds of a death or a divorce can cause a person to become critical or cynical, and being overly critical can be a sign of your partner's insecurities. If he or she sees only the bad in people and attacks their personhood instead of addressing the behavior alone, you may have a big problem later on, especially with children involved. Constructive or gentle correction is one thing, but being around a negative, pseudosuperior nitpicker is asking for a life of hurt, frustration, and disappointment.

10. Incompatibility. How different are your parenting styles, philosophies of stepparenting, backgrounds, lifestyles, values, educational levels, interests, and so on? If there is a great disparity in any of these areas, it may cause problems in your marriage later on, so work through any major differences before you marry. Make sure you are compatible in these important areas so that you don't end up living with an incompatibility for the rest of your life.

11. Personal habits. Does your partner have any habits that are diametrically opposed to your tastes, values, and desires? These may include smoking or drinking or even such minor irritants as bad table manners, sloppiness, poor hygiene, or even incessant gum chewing. Habits you may be able to ignore now may become a problem later on. Can you live with a man who refuses to discipline his children? Can you live with a woman who coddles her child to the point of letting him or her sleep in her bed? Anything from pet peeves to serious parenting or personality issues needs to be addressed.

12. Don't forget the kids. Even though we're focusing on marriage, children will dramatically affect your relationship, especially if they're against your marriage. Be sure your children are mentally and emotionally ready to accept your remarriage—and a stepparent—into their lives. If they aren't ready, seek the help of a pastor or other professional before proceeding with your marriage.

A "perfect score" in all categories is highly unlikely, but pay close attention to obvious or troublesome danger signs. The old adage "Let the buyer beware!" still applies, even when searching for a mate. All too often, people marry before they have enough information about their future spouse. They get caught up in the thrill of a new and exciting relationship and unintentionally forget to look deeper.

Even though we know that no one is perfect, we can often fool ourselves into thinking we've found a nearly perfect match. But the truth is, we all have bad habits and weaknesses, and we have to be realistic when we rate our future mates.

Establishing a healthy second marriage and blending a family has enough of its own unique challenges; it's unwise to complicate it with red flags you shouldn't overlook. Evaluate your relationship honestly and get help now if you need it. You'll be glad you did.

☙ BLENDING WITH KIDS

Are Your Kids Ready to Become a Blending Family?

Kids may seem resilient, and they can be, but it's important to keep in mind that when there is a death or a divorce, children are hurt as well, but in a different way. In the case of divorce, many children still dream of getting their divorced parents back together again, they may see a new marriage as a threat to their dream. Children may even try to sabotage your relationship, or they simply may not understand how a remarriage will change their family for the rest of their lives.

Do your children seem emotionally stable and able to laugh and love without a cloud of sadness, bitterness, or depression hanging over them? Have they had enough time with your future spouse so that they feel comfortable and safe with him or her? Do they have enough age-appropriate autonomy so they aren't insecure and overly dependent on you? If so, they may be ready to accept your remarriage and to blend as a family.

On the other hand, if they suffered some abuse in the past that they still need healing from, now is the time to work through these issues. If any of your children are acting out, or if you see signs of depression, anger, bitterness, or other negative emotions, it will affect your remarriage and your blending family if you don't deal with them now. Your children may simply need time to heal before you proceed with your second marriage.

A helpful resource for understanding children and the intricacies of blending a family is the book *Beyond the Brady Bunch: Hope and Help for Blended Families* by Ray and Debbie Alsdorf. They have lived through blending a family and can provide tools to help you through the process too.

❦ APPRAISING MY LIFE

List some of the most important qualities you bring to this marriage relationship.

How do these characteristics match up with your prospective mate?

Describe the five most important qualities you expect in a second marriage.

What specific characteristics or behaviors do you absolutely not want in a marriage partner?

What red flags, if any, do you need to deal with?

❧ ASSESSING OUR LIVES

Here are some important questions to discuss together:

1. What is true intimacy, and how can you achieve it as a couple?
2. What has each of you learned from your past relationships?
3. Do you both have a servant's heart? How do you show it?
4. How can each of you serve your partner better?

5. Does either of you have a pattern of negative, selfish behavior that concerns one or both of you?

6. Who has given you feedback about your relationship? What concerns do they have?

7. Is either of you rebounding from a relationship? If so, what healing needs to take place?

8. Does either of you seem emotionally unstable?

9. Does either of you feel uncomfortable with your singleness? Why? What does this say about you?

10. Does either of you have any kind of addiction? If so, what do you need to do about it individually and as a couple?

11. Does either of you have a history of abuse? If so, what do you need to do about it individually and as a couple?

12. Have you crossed a line sexually? If so, what are you going to do about it?

13. Do you share the same faith? Are you spiritually compatible?

14. Is either of you too critical?

15. Are you incompatible in any way as a couple (e.g., values, habits, beliefs, parenting styles, interests, etc.)?

16. Are any personal habits a problem for either of you?

17. Are there emotional, mental, or relational challenges with any of your children? If so, what do you need to do about it?

18. Is there any other emotional, physical, or financial baggage that either of you needs to know about?

19. What issues do you need to resolve before you marry?

You and your future spouse are seeking answers to some very tough questions. You may discover a problem and find that you can't move forward with your relationship until it has been resolved. That's okay. Better now than later! If you discover you're in a danger zone and need to put your relationship on hold or break it off, be kind and gentle but firm in your convictions, and then move on. Don't settle for anything but God's best!

❦ A MOMENT FOR FUN!

Take turns completing the following statements about your future mate. It's okay if you don't know every answer. Just use it as an opportunity to learn something new about each other.

Your birthday is . . .
Your favorite dessert is . . .
Your favorite movie is . . .
You grew up in the town of . . .
In college, you majored in . . .
Politically, you usually vote . . . (conservative, liberal, moderate)

❦ APPLYING GOD'S WORD

God's purpose for marriage is good. Ephesians 5:31 says, "For this reason a man will leave his father and mother and be united to his wife, and the two will become one flesh."

Growing spiritually is part of preparing yourselves to remarry. Your spiritual life is both personal and corporate. It's becoming more like Christ as He changes your thinking, attitudes, and actions. It takes a lifetime. It takes openness, honesty, and commitment.

Growing together spiritually involves talking about spiritual things, reading the Bible, and living what you learn. It's about praying together, studying God's Word together, worshipping together, and even serving together. It's about allowing God to change your behavior and your thinking patterns. It's being humble enough to acknowledge when you've done wrong and be willing to seek God together to help you get it right. It's an ever-growing, ever-learning adventure you can share together.

Growing together spiritually is an attitude of the heart—a heart that yearns after God and desires to be more like Him. You don't have to think exactly the same way about every topic; realize that people grow, change, and develop on their spiritual journeys.

Everything in your relationship becomes stronger when you make your spiritual relationship as a couple a priority. So continue to look inward and determine what healthy reasons cause you to want to be married to this particular person.

3

Trusting Again

What Do You Expect from a Second Marriage?

The expectations we have heading into a second marriage are often quite different from those of a first marriage. Our past experiences and our current circumstances can overshadow the bliss younger couples might have going into a first marriage. There might be issues of trust, safety, and security. A death or a divorce may result in a cynical, or at least cautious, view of the future. Knowing how these expectations can affect your marriage is important.

For both Susan and I (Dale), trust was a huge factor. But as I grew in my faith and healed from my past, I believed that I could trust again, if I could find a woman who was godly and trustworthy. For me, these key traits became paramount as I formed my expectations for a possible future mate. Susan had the same expectations; she wanted a godly and trustworthy man above all else.

Where do we get most of our expectations?

1. Our family of origin affects us greatly. For good or bad, parents are usually our biggest role models. Our siblings influence us too.

2. Our peers have a huge influence on what we expect of relationships, and so does our culture—the entertainment industry and the media. Both have a tremendous impact on our expectations of marriage and relationships.

3. In a second marriage, the biggest influence is often our previous marriage. Whether you lost a spouse through death or went through a divorce, there are usually some negative feelings you need to deal with. Grief over the loss, sadness, depression, anger, pain, hurt, and trauma—these emotions and feelings can often affect your expectations of a second marriage.

When Susan and I met with Tim and Hannah, we could quickly see that the hurts of Hannah's past caused her to project unfair expectations onto Tim. Thankfully, Hannah was wise enough to realize this and work toward letting go of her past so she could move forward with Tim.

"I had some unconscious expectations of Tim," Hannah says. "At first I expected that Tim would treat me badly, like my first husband, but that was unfair. I expected Tim to support us financially—because I had to do it all the first time around—and he did! I expected Tim to come home after work (my first husband would either go out with his friends or to a bar). And Tim not only comes home, but he wants to be with us."

Like Hannah, we all seek happiness and security. But how we achieve it varies with each of us. This, again, is where expectations come into play. What is fun for one person may not be fun for the other. What is hurtful or scary to one person may not affect the other.

Do you expect to freely spend money or save it for a rainy day? Do you expect your future spouse to do all the housework? What do you expect of your future mate as he or she stepparents your child? Because we are uniquely different from each other, we must understand one another's expectations if we're to have healthy relationships.

We all expect to experience love in our marriages, but what does a loving relationship look like through your eyes? Words like *commitment*, *honesty*, and *faithfulness* may come to mind. Like Hannah and Tim, each person might express love in different ways.

A man may show his love by working hard at his career, even at the expense of time with his wife and family. He may think he's showing love, but often his wife may not perceive it that way. Unknown or unexpressed expectations can often lead to trouble. So it's crucial that you and your future mate communicate your expectations of each other and your relationship, even though it will take a lot of work.

Shadows of the Past

Have you shared your expectations, hopes, dreams, and goals with your future mate? Too often we don't realize how these things can affect our marriage relationships. Hannah and Tim wish they had discussed these topics a lot more before they married.

Hannah married her first husband, Joe, while she was still in college. Because neither she nor Joe was really ready for marriage and the relationship wasn't built on a strong Christian foundation, their marriage was rough from the very beginning. Then a baby came along, and though Hannah expected to stay home and care for the baby, Joe expected her to keep working to support the family.

"The marriage got worse and worse," Hannah says. "I look back on it now, and I realize that I didn't respect Joe the way I should have. I see the wrong I did, but I couldn't stay in an abusive relationship. Just because someone doesn't leave bruises on you doesn't mean there isn't hurt. I gave everything I could give, but it wasn't enough. My baby, Alicia, was just thirteen months old when the marriage ended, and it was very hard."

Time passed and Hannah healed, and then she got reacquainted with Tim, a former college roommate of Hannah's brother. When they started dating and getting serious, Hannah didn't realize it, but some of the expectations she had for a future marriage were reflections of her first marriage.

Hannah was bringing old baggage, pain, and hurts, as well as a sense of failure from her first marriage, into her second. Some of the expectations were valid; some were unrealistic; some were based on the pain of the past. But thankfully she didn't let the unrealistic and unhealthy expectations define their marriage—and neither should you.

Unrealistic Expectations

Hannah's expectations for Tim to support his family and be home with them weren't wrong, but they were fear-based. If someone has been hurt by the betrayal of a former spouse, deep wounds may also cause him or her to form cynical or unrealistic expectations. We need to assess our past and the lies of our culture and the media, and look at what God says are holy expectations of relationships and marriage.

Which of these unrealistic and false messages about relationships might you believe, consciously or unconsciously?

- Relationships aren't meant to last.
- I can judge a person's character by his or her physical beauty, so I want a trophy wife or husband.
- Men just can't commit.
- Commitment isn't important or necessary.
- Wealth and material things bring happiness.
- Personal pleasure is the ultimate goal; boredom is bad and should be avoided; my pleasure is most important.
- Sexual experimentation is necessary to really know a person.
- Casual, premarital, or recreational sex is acceptable.
- Cohabitation is healthy and necessary.
- Using someone for my own sexual gratification is okay.
- Violence and sensuality are acceptable forms of entertainment.
- Pornography and promiscuity are pleasurable and natural.

Our culture has also perpetuated some unrealistic expectations that give people a false perception of marriage. Which of the following perceptions have you heard people express?

- Marriage is a fifty-fifty proposition.
- I'm sure I can change him or her.
- I will be complete and fulfilled in marriage.
- We will be able to read each other's minds and know what to expect.
- Marriage will solve most of my problems.
- Nothing will ever change.
- Differences don't matter.
- Sex will always be great.
- I'll always feel in love.
- Our families will always understand and support our choices.
- Money will solve all our problems.
- Stepparenting will be a breeze.
- Blending a family will be easy.

When you don't understand what is expected in a relationship, lots of conflict, stress, and frustration can arise. What's really important to each of you spiritually, physically, educationally, financially, emotionally, and sexually? What do you expect your new family to be like? What about the children? What role do you expect your future spouse to take regarding stepparenting?

Susan and I (Dale) spent a lot of time discussing our expectations. Because we'd been hurt in the past and had been single for so long, we knew that our previous experiences could affect us greatly if we didn't understand each other well. Knowing our faults and foibles helped us both adjust more easily to the relational mishaps that would come our way.

How does your future mate feel about playful banter, jokes, or surprises? Dale makes me (Susan) laugh every day with his witty quips and comebacks. But because of my past experiences, surprises and sarcasm don't always sit well with me. Surprising each other is one of those tricky expectations that sometimes doesn't work out the way you hope, as Hannah also realized.

"Our last Valentine's Day didn't work out quite right," Hannah shares with us. "I took all the kids and got some things to decorate Tim's office, but he wasn't too impressed."

Tim says, "I was in my work zone, and it got complicated. Because of the office policies, Hannah couldn't bring the kids up to my office, and I didn't have time to deal with it all, so it didn't go well. She wasn't too happy when I got home."

"But we celebrated Valentine's the next night," Hannah says. "It turned out well, but there will always be misunderstandings and expectations that get in the way. You just have to work it out!"

Hannah's right! As you learn about each other's priorities and preferences, you'll be able to better understand each other's expectations. And as you explore your expectations, you'll begin to realize how comfortable or uncomfortable you might be with your future mate's expectations of you.

Extended-Family Expectations

"It was important for us to do premarital counseling," Tim said. "But I don't remember talking about expectations very much. I wish we had, because one family's expectations were almost the exact opposite from the other family's, so that was a huge challenge. Hannah has always been around her large extended family, but my family wasn't close to or engaged with our extended family. My family was closed and rather controlling, so Hannah didn't understand my parents' expectations."

"Tim's parents were worried because I had been married before and had a daughter," Hannah says. "Tim had never been married and is really close with his parents. So even after we married, they expected to still be an authority in his life. His mom and I would clash a lot, and it took a long time for us to trust each other. It took time, but eventually we worked things out." Because of Hannah and Tim's determination to communicate and work through these expectations, trust has been built between them and their marriage strengthened.

"My parents expected us to be with them every Christmas," Tim says, "which wasn't realistic. I wish we would've anticipated those extended-family expectations earlier on." (We'll take a closer look at dealing with family issues in chapter 10.)

"My ex never wanted me to be with my extended family," Hannah says, "so I put negative expectations on Tim and thought he would respond the same way as my first husband. I would be defensive, and then I was surprised when Tim responded differently. Tim encourages relationships with my family, and that's such a relief to me."

"I never had many traditions in my family," Tim says, "so we like to make new ones—like cutting down a Christmas tree every year. We also like to show our kids a good mix of cultural experiences—city life as well as country life."

"When it comes to Alicia, my ex and I have a rotating schedule for Christmas and Thanksgiving," Hannah says. "We tried passing her back and forth halfway through Christmas Day, but we all hated that. So now we just have two Christmas days. When Alicia is with her dad and not with us on December 25, it's a little sad, but I hang on to the fact that I'll see her and celebrate with her the very next day!"

"Making time for each other, apart from the rest of the family, is also an important expectation for Tim and I," Hannah says. "Once a year we go away together, and on Friday nights, we do something special together." In a busy blending family, time together without kids or extended family is vital to making a second marriage strong.

Financial Expectations

Money is one of the greatest stressors in most marriages, but in second marriages it can be that much more challenging. It's extremely important to talk about your financial expectations, goals, dreams, and plans. (We'll deal with this further in chapter 8.) Sometimes it's easy to carry over money troubles from your past marriage. Hannah did just that. Early in their marriage, whenever Tim tried to develop a budget and work on their finances with her, Hannah resisted.

"Although we talked about our money expectations a little before we got married," Tim says, "we just didn't have a good long-term plan. So after we married, I tried to figure it out."

"I thought he was trying to control me," Hannah admitted, "but now I know that Tim just wanted us to get out of debt and be responsible. Early on I thought he was trying to blame me for spending money."

"It took a long time for Hannah to realize that I wasn't attacking her," Tim says. "Because of the experiences she had before, I had to show her that she was safe with me and that we could work together. She had to accept the idea that we're a team."

"When you both have the same expectations," Hannah says, "it's amazing what you can do. Because of this, we don't fight about money anymore. We also realized that childcare was getting too expensive, so we decided that I should quit work, stay home, and care for the kids. Now we live on one income, and that's a new adjustment—with new expectations."

Parenting Expectations

What are your expectations about having and raising children? For many second-marriage couples, this is a challenging topic. One or both of you may be bringing children into the marriage, and you may be hesitant about adding yet another child. Or you may be excited about having a baby together. Whatever the case may be, talk through all your parenting expectations before you marry.

If one of you doesn't have children, this may be extra challenging,

Tips for Meeting Each Other's Expectations and Making Your Marriage Strong

When you discover that one or both of you have conflicting expectations, choose to solve these differences through kind and respectful communication.

- Articulate your expectations so your partner understands what you need.
- Assess each other's expectations to see if they're realistic, and choose to adjust them accordingly.
- Realize that both of you need to grow and develop into your own blended way of doing things.
- Expect that commitment and compromise mean giving up some things to get others.
- Try to respond kindly to each other's valid expectations, even when you don't agree with them or when they're different from your own.
- Expect that change is a given. You don't have to be stuck in the way you've always done something. Find new ways that work for both of you.
- Be humble, unselfish, and flexible.
- Forsake all others and do what's best for your relationship.
- Set reasonable goals, make plans, and dream together.
- Leave the past behind, including certain obligations to your families and friends.
- Determine to become a family God will be proud of.

especially if you're a woman. As a new bride, you'll be instantly sharing your husband with his children, and you may experience feelings of resentment, jealousy, or insecurity. But also understand that this is a huge change for the children too. Though this transition is a challenging one whether you're a woman or a man, if you go into it knowing that it's a critical season in your family's life, and if you determine to be understanding, patient, and loving, this season can build a strong foundation for healthy relationships all the way around.

Will one of you stay home and care for the children, or will both of you work outside the home? How many children would you like to have together? How will you treat your children versus his or hers? How will stepparenting work? How do you feel about adoption?

"One of the things that attracted me to Tim was that I knew he'd be a really good dad to Alicia, and we talked about having more children," Hannah says. "Despite the fact that I knew I could trust Tim to treat me and Alicia well and make good decisions, I kept expecting that history would repeat itself. I thought he'd yell at me, but he never did. I thought he'd be mean, but he never was. Even after we were married, I expected negative things from him."

Tim understood Hannah's painful past, so he worked with her to build trust and make her feel safe and secure—and he wanted to prove her expectations were wrong! "Although I was unaware of her false expectations," Tim says, "I knew she needed me to show her I was safe."

Today Hannah and Tim have three children—Alicia from Hannah's first marriage and two together. And now they're even talking about adoption! The healing Hannah has experienced because of Tim's love, patience, and understanding has made all the difference.

One of the greatest adventures of marriage, and sometimes one of the biggest surprises or uncertainties of your journey together, relates to having children and stepchildren. God has a beautiful plan called family, and that plan is important to Him. There is nothing more rewarding than raising children, whether they are his, hers, or yours together. After all, according to God, starting a family is one of the reasons for marrying (Genesis 1:28)!

Realistic Expectations

"Commitment is a realistic expectation to have," Tim says. "Hannah and I are both committed, and we show it by our actions. We won't give up. We'll do whatever it takes to make our marriage work. Love is great, but you don't always feel it. When you're committed, you do what it takes to prove your love. There's nothing I won't do to make our marriage work."

"We try to be flexible and willing to compromise," Hannah adds, "and we try to treat each other unselfishly and accept life as it comes."

Hannah and Tim are wise! God expects you to fully commit to the one He gives you as your mate, and He wants you to find that lifelong commitment to be one of the most redemptive aspects of life.

Like Hannah, both Dale and I (Susan) have experienced the healing and hope that only comes with this kind of committed relationship. And knowing that each of us is unwavering in our commitment to each other makes all the difference. We believe that a healthy second marriage highlights God's grace as we heal from our pasts, find true companionship, experience real intimacy, and reflect His glory in our relationship.

As you move toward marriage, keep in mind that God expects you to serve each other unselfishly; accept one another's unique personalities, needs, and differences; and be faithful to each other throughout your entire lives. God also expects you to love each other unconditionally, be merciful and forgiving, and be patient as you learn and grow together.

What about the realistic expectations you may have individually? Each of you has goals, dreams, and expectations that may be very different from your future mate's. That's normal. The keys to merging these expectations successfully are communication, compromise, and care. Continually ask yourself, "What's best for our relationship? What's really important to us as a couple?"

"Tim is a good man," Hannah says. "He's very forgiving, kind, and loving. So I try to meet his needs, figure out how I can give back to him, and show him that I love him. We try to serve each other, and we try to give to each other. It's not about me; it's about us! Tim comes home and helps with the house, the cooking, and the kids. He would never expect me to carry all the responsibility."

Though their journey has had its ups and downs, Hannah and Tim have learned what each other's expectations are and figured out how to meet them. This couple has matured, grown together, and overcome the challenges of a second marriage with honesty, maturity, flexibility, and a positive attitude. And because they meet each challenge with commitment, understanding, and love, they enjoy a fruitful and fulfilling marriage.

⚘ BLENDING WITH KIDS

What about the Kids' Expectations in a Blending Family?
For kids and stepparents alike, adjusting to a second marriage is no easy task. But if you work at it from a foundation of love, respect, and acceptance, you'll be okay. Though it often takes years to come to a satisfying and stable place, you can do it!

The expectations children might have for a second marriage can be mixed. Kids often feel like they are losing out, or they're confused as to where they fit, where the stepparent fits, and whether the biological parent will maintain the same relationship with them. Though they may be happy that they have a "new" parent, they may also feel that he or she is an intruder. Hang in there; keep your expectations realistic, and don't be disappointed if the process is slow. Remember that it's a season of change, and change isn't easy.

"Kids pick up on our expectations of what marriage is—and of what we expect of them," Tim says. "They expect whatever they see. For instance, Hannah and I hold hands when we're together, so the kids expect that. If they don't see it, they wonder what's wrong. It's important to model what we expect from them—such as kindness and respect."

"I love that Tim takes his father role seriously. This week he's going to start the tradition of taking Alicia on 'dates,'" Hannah says. "They're going to get all dressed up, and Tim is going to come to the door and ask Alicia out! It'll be fun, and it's great to see their relationship deepen."

As the stepparent feels the stress of adjusting to his or her new role, the biological parent can help ease the way.

"For the person who's been married before, don't compare your present spouse to the former one," Hannah suggests. "That's not fair or smart. See your marriage as a new and fresh start, and go easy on everyone. Empower the new parent to take a parental role gently and gradually; otherwise the kids will feel that your spouse isn't a part of the family. I tended to be defensive of Alicia at first, but as Tim built trust and adjusted to his role as a dad, we now share parenting really well."

Just as no two people think alike, no two parents approach parenting the same way. And for the spouse who hasn't been a parent before, it's extra challenging. Add to that the reality that the stepparent and stepchild are unrelated, and the best thing you can all do is relax, respect and accept one another, and don't force the process. Remember that you're on a journey together.

"I really didn't know what to expect," Tim says. "Never having been married before, I had to adjust to family life. Having a stepdaughter wasn't a problem. But what I didn't realize was how much I'd have to deal with the ex stuff. I knew, theoretically, that we'd have to deal with it, but emotionally it's hard."

Tim and Hannah had to figure out what it looked like to parent together. "As a stepfather, I think there's only so much I can do to discipline

Alicia," Tim says. "I've never given her a spanking, and though I feel more free with our biological children, she's still in my care."

"Tim can give Alicia a really stern talk, and that'll do it," Hannah adds. "Tim's so gentle with her, and he always comes from a place of love. I think that makes all the difference."

Tim was wise to let Hannah take the disciplinary role as Alicia adjusted to his place in her life. Though he wanted the full identity of being her stepdad, he knew that she had to set the pace. "Now Alicia happily tells others that she has two dads and two moms," Tim says.

Dale and I (Susan) agree that letting the biological parent take the lead is critical regarding discipline. A stepparent should let the biological parent have complete responsibility for the discipline of his or her child for the first season of their blending family life. Gradually, as the child bonds and feels safe with the stepparent, gentle verbal discipline might become a part of the stepparenting journey.

Hannah told us, "When our three-year-old, Angie, recently asked me where *her* stepdad was, we realized that Alicia views having a stepdad as a good thing, as a badge of honor and status, and that really shows!"

But even this can be a challenge when the other parent makes it hard. "Alicia called Tim 'Dad,' until Joe, my ex-husband, made her feel bad about it," Hannah says. "Joe told Alicia that it hurt his feelings when she called Tim 'Dad.' So now Alicia doesn't know what to do."

"But I can be her other dad without having the title," Tim says. "It's how we interact that's more important to us. Alicia treats me like her dad, and I see her as my daughter."

Although there are challenges, the rewards are great. But in the midst of parenting and stepparenting, never put your marriage on the back burner. To have a successful, thriving, vibrant, and intimate marriage and family life, remember that your marriage must always remain your top priority, even when the demands of children vie for its place of prominence.

Far too many marriages have disintegrated by focusing on the children and ignoring the marriage, and that's a disastrous mistake for all concerned. Don't let this happen to you. If you read books and learn all you can about marriage and parenting, you'll help to keep your marriage vibrant, even through the challenges you'll face as parents in a blending family. Never stop growing in your relationship, and love your children out of the abundance of your love for each other.

🌱 APPRAISING MY LIFE

What are your expectations as a couple regarding the following topics? After each of you thinks about your own expectations, discuss them together.

- Where do you want to live?
- What are your home expectations?
- How do you think you should parent as a couple?
- How would you like to spend your time together?
- What about visiting extended family?
- What about time with friends?
- What about vacations?
- What about your career?
- What about church and religious life?
- What about hobbies, recreational activities, sports?
- How should you and your partner handle finances?
- How do you like to celebrate holidays?
- What do you expect of your partner as far as disciplining and raising your child as a stepparent?

🌱 ASSESSING OUR LIVES

Now it's time to talk about what you both expect regarding the division of household chores, errands, tasks, and duties. Be sure to include the children. Discuss each of these topics, and any others that may come up. (We'll discuss this further in chapter 11.)

Who will do the following chores, and what can be done together?
- cooking and preparing the meals
- cleaning up after meals
- cleaning the kitchen
- cleaning bathrooms
- cleaning other parts of the house
- keeping things tidy
- taking out the trash
- doing the laundry
- shopping
- handling the budget and bills
- decorating
- taking care of house repairs
- maintaining the car
- doing the yard work
- planning trips
- planning nights out
- giving gifts
- planning and shopping for holidays
- handling correspondence
- caring for children
- enforcing family rules
- caring for aging parents

🌱 A MOMENT FOR FUN!

What do you think God is calling you to do?

Imagine you could go on a cruise anywhere in the world. Where would it be and why?

🌱 APPLYING GOD'S WORD

Godly expectations come from a heart and mind that seek to be like Christ. As we understand what He expects of us, we can learn to be more like Him. Reading 2 Peter 1:3–8 together is a great place to start:

> His divine power has given us everything we need for life and godliness through our knowledge of him who called us by his own glory and goodness. Through these he has given us his very great and precious promises, so that through them you may participate in the divine nature and escape the corruption in the world caused by evil desires.
>
> For this very reason, make every effort to add to your faith goodness; and to goodness, knowledge; and to knowledge, self-control; and to self-control, perseverance; and to perseverance, godliness; and to godliness, brotherly kindness; and to brotherly kindness, love. For if you possess these qualities in increasing measure, they will keep you from being ineffective and unproductive.

Here are a few other scriptures that will help you develop healthy expectations:

> We take captive every thought to make it obedient to Christ.
> (2 Corinthians 10:5)

Do not be deceived: God cannot be mocked. A man reaps what he sows. The one who sows to please his sinful nature, from that nature will reap destruction. (Galatians 6:7–8)

Do not love the world or anything in the world. (1 John 2:15)

4

Serving Each Other

How Can You Meet Each Other's Needs?

After Rick and Linda got engaged, deciding on the house where they would live quickly became a major issue that required a lot of discussion. Although each of them already had a house, they realized that neither place would work well for them as a couple. Ideally they wanted to build a new house, but that would only be possible if they sold their separate houses. When the houses didn't sell, Rick and Linda had to make some tough choices.

They married and moved into Linda's house, knowing it was a temporary fix. When five months passed and the houses still hadn't sold, Rick began talking about how he could renovate his house and make it into a house that Linda would enjoy and be comfortable in. She was hesitant for two reasons: She wasn't sure Rick had the skills to do a major remodel, and she had never seen a successful remodel. So these were unknowns that concerned her.

"Though we didn't have the emotional issues of the exes having lived in either house like many second-marriage couples do, we both liked our own houses but not the other's," Rick says. "We wanted to do what was right and not let our emotional ties to our homes interfere with our decisions, so I listed the advantages and disadvantages of each house and tried to analyze it all without our personal feelings getting in the way."

"Then one night when we were talking about what to do," Linda recalls, "Rick held out his hands and said, 'I want to use these hands while I can.' I realized that doing this renovation was a deep and important need for Rick, and it melted my heart. I realized I just had to put my trust in him."

So Linda agreed, and they let the dream of building a new house go. Linda chose to meet Rick's need to work with his hands; Rick chose to meet Linda's need for a home she'd love. They launched into a major remodeling project, and they did it together. Now they have a home they both love and enjoy together.

I (Susan) also had to adjust to moving from the new house I had built just a year earlier to Dale's home. Though his was a beautiful custom home he had personally designed, he had also been a bachelor for nearly two decades, and his decor reflected that. But I was amazed—and oh so grateful—that he wanted me to help make his house our home together, and during our first year of marriage, we found our blended style and made our home a place that we consider equally ours.

It's important to understand the needs you and your future spouse have and to discern the differences between wants or desires and real needs. This can help you know how to meet your future mate's needs. Since unmet needs can cause a lot of frustration, misunderstanding, and conflict in a marriage, we want to help you avoid some of those pitfalls.

Once you recognize the specific needs each of you has, you can then communicate and work toward meeting them. If you know how to successfully meet each other's needs, you'll develop a strong second marriage that will be satisfying and fulfilling.

Needs Versus Wants

The difference between a need and a want is often difficult to discern. The marketing media say that we "need" everything they advertise, and we need it now! They can confuse us into thinking that a *want* is really a *need*.

Because Linda has chronic myofascial pain as well as degenerative arthritis in her knees, she can no longer work outside the home. In her previous marriage, this would have led to verbal abuse. Not so with Rick.

"Rick has never complained," Linda says. "He financially provides for me more than I ever could have imagined. He is sympathetic and has done lots of things to meet my needs both physically and emotionally. For example, he installed sliding shelves because I can't kneel or squat. He runs basement errands because the stairs hurt my knees. He helps with the chores that hurt me physically and massages my arms when they ache. Talk about fulfilling needs! He gets the grand prize in my world."

For each couple, there are different wants or needs (big and small) that must be negotiated. Making healthy decisions for your marriage will often require setting aside wants in order to meet legitimate needs. And when kids and all their needs are involved, it very often requires a lot of sacrifice—from everybody!

For Dale and me (Susan), our needs are more emotional than material. I need to feel safe and secure, and Dale needs to feel respected and appreciated. So Dale works hard to assure me that I'm safe with him and secure in our relationship, while I make sure to appreciate and respect him in all he does. This way we serve each other and meet each other's deepest needs, thus deepening our love for one another.

That's why it's so important to identify your real needs as individuals and as a couple. And then there are the needs of your children! Taking a long-term view of blending-family life and working from there is an important first step. Then choosing daily to unselfishly meet each other's needs—and giving grace when one of you falls short—is another critical component.

Wants

Beyond wanting material things, there are also wants and desires that masquerade as needs. We may think it's our right to have our needs met first and foremost—instead of serving the other person. Kids are especially good at feeling this way! We might think we need to be in control or have others do things our way, so we demand, dominate, or manipulate situations to get our "needs" met. We may think we need to have a good time even when we can't afford it, or see an inappropriate movie even when it goes against our morals. Sometimes we don't even realize that those selfish desires can lead to addictions and other destructive habits that may alienate our family or destroy our marriage.

For Rick and Linda, both of their first marriages were destroyed by this very problem. Linda's husband was narcissistic—everything was about meeting his needs, including his gambling and sexual addictions. For Rick, his first wife left him for another man who she thought would meet her needs better than Rick could. Rick was faced with the responsibility of caring for his kids alone. I'm sure many of you have similar stories.

Unless you understand the difference between a want or desire and a valid, legitimate need, you'll continually struggle with fulfilling your mate's needs—and being fulfilled—in a healthy way.

Needs

Each of us has unique needs, and our past experiences influence those needs. But God also gave us universal needs. First, we need Him. God has the answers to help us clearly understand both our loved one's needs and our own. He can also guide us in knowing how to meet the deepest needs of our spouses.

Second, we need each other. Since marriage is the most intimate relationship of all, none of us can be a loner or be emotionally withdrawn without it adversely affecting our partner. Genesis 2:18 says, "The LORD God said, 'It is not good for the man to be alone. I will make a helper suitable for him.'" He created us to need each other, and when we understand God's plan for us, we can become that suitable helper for each other.

Third, we have personal needs. Some are physical or emotional; others are spiritual or social. The problem is that we get mixed up as to what's really an important and valid need and what's a personal desire—something we think we need because it's been imposed on us by marketing, the media, or the world's standards. Figuring all this out is important if we are to meet legitimate needs and let go of unnecessary desires.

We also have basic human needs, such as the need for food, clothing, shelter, and safety. And there are other God-given needs as well—to be loved and respected, just to name two. For Dale and me (Susan), love and respect are certainly important needs for us.

There are many possible needs unique to each of you, so how can you be sure you know and meet your future mate's deepest and most important needs, and frankly, whose needs comes first? Philippians 2:3–4 says, "Do nothing out of selfish ambition or vain conceit, but in humility consider others better than yourselves. Each of you should look not only to your own interests, but also to the interests of others." It's simple: Your attitude and the choices you make really do matter.

This scripture encourages us to have a servant's heart, to have a determination to serve our spouses while putting our needs behind theirs and often behind the needs of our children as well. Jesus spent His life serving others; the Bible is filled with stories of how He served people by healing the sick, feeding the multitudes, even washing His disciples' feet. Then He provided the ultimate service: He gave His life for us all. He set the standard for us to emulate, and whenever two people choose to selflessly serve each other, the peace, contentment, satisfaction, and love they experience is like nothing else.

Emotional Needs

Though we can never expect our future spouses to meet all our needs, we can assess our needs and communicate them to our partners. First we have to figure out if our needs are valid or are just selfish desires. Understanding the underlying feelings, experiences, pain, or scars that developed those needs can help us to be conscious, compassionate, and better able to meet those needs.

Emotional hurts from past relationships can affect our needs more than we realize. "Because I had an unfaithful husband, I have a great need to know that Rick will be faithful," Linda admits. "So when I get insecure, we talk about my fears, and he'll reassure me."

"Linda always wants to talk things through," Rick says. "Adjusting to having more conflict in our discussions, instead of holding back, was hard for me. But I've learned to work through things, especially because resolving conflict and having open communication is so important to her."

"My ex was very self-absorbed; everything was about him," Linda says, "so my needs were rarely met. With Rick, even though we both make mistakes, I know he'll do all he can to meet whatever need I have."

"Linda needs me to communicate and reassure her regularly," Rick says. "She needs more affirmation than I do. With all the physical and emotional changes of both of us growing older and of her having hurts from the past, I want to be aware of her emotional needs. Sometimes it's best if she just tells me what she needs."

"A few weeks ago, I was feeling insecure about some things," Linda says. "I needed to know that I was beautiful to him. Rick did one better; he told me he *cherished* our relationship, and that filled my love bucket to overflowing!

"Rick needs my respect and admiration," Linda continues, "and he's a tender man, so I need to be very careful and gentle when I'm emotional about something. If I'm not, it takes him days to recover. Also, Rick has been open with me about his need for 'guy time' and time to work with his hands. Keeping open communication about what we need really helps us."

Each person's emotional needs change over time, so you'll need to adjust as the years go by. That's part of the joy in the lifetime journey of remarriage. You'll also make some mistakes along the way, and that's okay. If you accept the fact that mistakes are part of the journey and will happen now and then, you'll be free to grow closer.

There will also be seasons in your marriage when you'll need to sacrifice some of your own needs for the good of your spouse or your kids. When you choose to do this, your relationship will deepen and become stronger through the trials of life. Respecting your husband even when he doesn't deserve it, or loving your wife even when it's not comfortable or convenient are two tangible ways to make that happen.

Unmet Needs

There are times when we fail, when we make mistakes, or when one of us has a need our partner either doesn't know how to meet or isn't responsible to meet. We should realize that only God can meet some of our needs. And when we understand that perfect love and unconditional acceptance can only be found in a relationship with Him, we achieve balance in our lives.

On their fifth anniversary, Rick and Linda went camping to celebrate. But they also decided that it was time for a marriage tune-up. "We had been so busy with life," Linda says, "that all of a sudden, I realized there was an ache in my heart. There were things we needed to talk about, but there didn't seem to be the right opportunity. So months went by, and I forgot about those things, or I stuffed them away. And we never quite found the time to have a good, healthy discussion. This time away gave us the chance to intentionally stop, reevaluate our relationship, and take the time to tune up our marriage. We spent five hours talking about our needs, and it was great!"

"We simply had to rekindle our awareness of each other's needs," Rick says, "and then we had to be willing to figure out how to meet those needs. People often go along in their marriage, and they get lazy. We forget to be deliberate about serving each other and keeping our marriage healthy."

"We were sliding into complacency," Linda says. "Often, it's simply being considerate of the other's feelings. If the wife has a concern or fear, for example, the husband should try to alleviate those concerns, and vice versa. And it's so important not to assume the other person just 'knows' what your need is."

"A person can get irritated when he or she doesn't get a need met," Rick adds. "But sometimes it's because that person hasn't told his or her spouse what that need is! We can't expect someone else to read our mind."

"Sometimes I hesitate to tell Rick about a need because I think it might spoil the moment," Linda says. "It doesn't feel as romantic to tell him I need romance. Especially since I think he should already know this. But then if he doesn't meet that need, I get disappointed and resentful and frustrated. I know that's not fair to him."

As Rick and Linda attest, unmet needs do cause conflict, frustration, and misunderstandings in a relationship. But learning how to keep short accounts, stay on top of things, and alleviate those misunderstandings can sure help.

Spiritual Needs

One of the keys to establishing a great second marriage is recognizing the spiritual needs of each other and encouraging your spouse to grow in his or her relationship with God. This may mean that you sacrifice an evening together so she can go to a ladies' Bible-study meeting. Or you decide not to buy a new dress so that he can afford to attend a men's retreat. Maybe you need to learn how to pray together or commit to reading God's Word together. Whatever your spiritual needs might be, talk about them before marrying and find out how you can help to meet each other's needs. Modeling a united spiritual life to your children is important as well. The truth is that enjoying spiritual intimacy together will give you a measure of success, satisfaction, and peace that other marriages that don't prioritize faith won't have.

For Susan and me (Dale), this was a big concern. Susan had been a Christian for several decades; I had been a true believer for only a few years. But she quickly realized that I was determined to live my life for God, and I relaxed about not having the years of biblical understanding that she did. Since before our wedding day, we've worked hard to become one spiritually, and it's been a great journey.

On a deep level, when you marry you "become one" (Genesis 2:24), and that has a spiritual component to it. Whether you recognize it or not, you long to be spiritually connected to each other, and unless you cultivate that connection, there will always be an emptiness, an unfulfilled part of your relationship.

From the very beginning, Rick and Linda chose to make their relationship a spiritually strong one. "We were very much on the same page spiritually, so this area was a strength for us," Rick says. "We don't always agree on every detail of our spiritual walk, but that's okay."

"I respect his opinion on things even when I don't agree," Linda says. "But from the very beginning, we decided that it was essential for us to take some time first thing every morning to read the Bible and pray together. Although that doesn't always happen, the majority of the time it does. It builds a special intimacy between us."

"This is probably the single greatest thing that's made our relationship strong," Rick says.

Rick and Linda enjoy attending church and leading a small group with couples who are real and transparent and with whom they can grow together spiritually. These activities are a part of meeting their spiritual needs as a remarried couple.

What are your spiritual needs, and how can each of you help ensure that those needs are met? First, find a church and commit to attend regularly. Next, pray together. For some couples, this isn't easy, but start by saying a prayer before meals. Then you can learn to pray at other times and for other things—for safety on a trip, for God's will, and to know His plan for your marriage.

Third, plan to grow spiritually together throughout your married life. After you marry, join a Bible study or small group with newly remarried couples with whom you can "do life" together. If your current church doesn't have a group, start one!

Fourth, find another second-marriage couple (whom you admire and respect) and ask them to mentor you. Meet with that couple every other week or once per month. Be honest, transparent, and inquisitive. Ask them how to deal with issues you're encountering. Seek their advice on struggles you may have. And be accountable to them for your Christian walk as a couple as well as individually.

Fifth, but possibly the most important, maintain your covenant commitment to God and to each other. Choose daily to maintain and develop your walk with God through faithfully growing in His ways. It's not always easy, but who expects that everything should be easy?

Finally, realize that as you grow and mature spiritually, these needs will change. Life is ever changing, and so is your spiritual life.

Other Needs

Obviously, we have many other needs as we discussed earlier—emotional needs, such as feeling accepted, valued, needed, and supported, or physical needs, such as being healthy, cared for, and safe. We have intellectual and educational needs, such as finding meaning in our work and having healthy self-esteem. We have social needs, such as having a sense of belonging, enjoying sexual intimacy with our spouses, and maintaining same-sex friendships. And intertwined in it all is the need for financial security.

"Linda has a great need for social interaction, so she takes the lead on planning and arranging our social life," Rick says. "Getting together with our family and our small group are two regular events for us. I know Linda needs social interaction, so I go along for the ride. I don't need it as much as she does, but I don't discourage her from connecting with others. In fact, she gets energized by it, so that's a plus for me."

"When we were doing our premarital counseling," Linda adds, "this issue came up. Rick's comment was that he'd do everything he can to accommodate that need. He's been wonderful and is very supportive, and he's such a servant in making our social events happen. He even enjoys our get-togethers—once they are happening."

For Rick and Linda, having a servant-minded attitude and being willing to make adjustments when needed are two ways they continually work to keep their second marriage strong. Linda says, "I have such gratitude for this man that I ask God to show me how I can bless him each and every day. I want to serve him, and I respect him, and I want to meet his needs—whatever they may be."

☙ BLENDING WITH KIDS

What about Family and Children's Needs?

When there are kids in the home, it's often critical for you as a couple to take a long-term view of blending-family life. Yes, in the short term, you'll probably be sacrificing many of your wants and desires—and sometimes even your needs—so you can meet the needs of your children. But it's important to keep the end in mind; one day your kids will be grown and moving on, and then you'll have greater freedom to make more personal choices as a couple.

As a second-marriage couple, be sure to talk about what this might look like. One of you may have a highly needy child at home; the other might not. One of you may strongly feel that every need your child has should supersede your spouse's or your own needs, while the other might not. Both of you may have severely needy kids who will require a lot of you and your second marriage.

How will you maintain a healthy marriage with these kinds of pressures and sacrifices? Although you must always keep your marriage relationship the top priority, self-sacrifice is often imperative during this season of blending-family life, so it's important to plan for these challenges. Talk about all this openly and honestly now so you'll avoid surprises later.

In reality, in a blending-family situation, so much of your success will come down to the attitude you have toward facing and overcoming the issues that arise, including meeting each other's needs. "I think that good will is huge," Linda says. "Rick and I desire to bless each other, and we want to fulfill each other's needs. Sometimes those include the needs of each other's children—and grandchildren!"

"We don't measure or keep score to see who's done more," Rick says. "We just serve."

"Because I see so much integrity and character in Rick, I really encourage his interaction with my sons," Linda says. "His example is important; he's a great role model for them. And he doesn't have to be 'the dad' to make a difference. He just draws them into his world and shows them how to be men of integrity. As he mentors them, he meets my need to see my sons have a good example in their lives."

As you can tell, there's a lot to this blending-family journey.

APPRAISING MY LIFE

In his classic book on marriage *His Needs, Her Needs*, Willard Harley says that many men and women have different top-five needs. Though your list may be different, here's a good starting point for discussion:

His needs:

- Sexual fulfillment—he can't do without it!
- Companionship—he needs a playmate.
- Attractive spouse—he needs a good-looking wife, to have his wife care about her appearance and make an effort to be attractive.
- Domestic support—he needs a place of peace and quiet.
- Admiration—he needs her to be proud of him.

Her needs:

- Affection—she can't do without it!
- Communication—she needs him to talk to her.
- Honesty—she needs to trust him completely.
- Financial support—she needs enough to live comfortably.
- Family commitment—she needs him to be a good family man.

"The husband and wife who commit themselves to meet each other's needs will lay a foundation for lifelong happiness in marriage that is deeper and more satisfying than they ever dreamed possible," Harley says.[1]

It's now time to assess your personal needs. Take some time to define each need and assess how much you need each one, personally, on a scale of one to five (one being the least important; five being the most important). You may even want to assess and rate the needs of your children.

Though many of these concepts overlap, the words will trigger emotions that will reveal your individual hot-button issues. This will help you understand your most important needs, and those of your future spouse and kids. Once you've recognized what your needs are, then you can discuss the needs of your future mate, as well as practical ways to meet them.

I need to feel . . .	Him	Her
Like I'm a priority	_____	_____
Like we're a team	_____	_____
Accepted	_____	_____
Wanted	_____	_____
Valued	_____	_____
Needed	_____	_____
Understood	_____	_____
Affirmed	_____	_____
Appreciated	_____	_____
Supported	_____	_____

I need . . .		
Love	_____	_____
Affection	_____	_____
Attention	_____	_____
Regular communication	_____	_____
Romance	_____	_____
Tenderness	_____	_____
Respect	_____	_____
Financial security	_____	_____
Safety	_____	_____
Trust	_____	_____
Dependability	_____	_____
Honesty	_____	_____
Companionship	_____	_____
Humility	_____	_____
Patience	_____	_____
Admiration	_____	_____
Forgiveness	_____	_____
Exclusivity	_____	_____
Commitment	_____	_____

I need . . .	Him	Her
Faithfulness	_____	_____
Sexual fulfillment	_____	_____
Security	_____	_____
Affirmation	_____	_____
Support	_____	_____
Devotion	_____	_____
Caring	_____	_____
Validation	_____	_____
Reassurance	_____	_____
Approval	_____	_____
Support	_____	_____
Encouragement	_____	_____
Quality time	_____	_____

☙ ASSESSING OUR LIVES

Each of you take turns naming three needs from the lists in the previous section that you think your future mate might not recognize as a need you have. Discuss how you can meet each other's needs in practical ways. Name three specific things you can start doing.

Now discuss these questions together:

- Are both of you Christians? How important is your faith to you? To your future mate?
- What are your spiritual needs as far as your involvement in a church? What does your partner need?
- What are your needs regarding prayer? (When you're married, would you like to pray before meals, at bedtime, in the morning, at other times?)
- How important is Bible reading to you? (Do you believe the Bible is the Word of God? Is daily study important to you? Is joining a Bible study with others something you want to do?)

- How important is spiritual leadership to you? Do you believe husbands should be the spiritual leaders of the home? Or that both of you, working together, should lead your family spiritually?
- Do you believe that marriage is a sacred covenant that shouldn't be broken?
- Do you believe that children are a gift from God?
- What religious traditions are important to you (e.g., baptism, communion, church membership, evangelism, celebrating Christmas and Easter, etc.)?
- Do you believe forgiveness is imperative and a regular part of life?
- Do you believe that God will help you in your marriage?

🌱 A MOMENT FOR FUN!

What was the best road trip you've ever taken?

Imagine having an extra hour in the day. What would you do with it?

🌱 APPLYING GOD'S WORD

When you meet your future mate's needs, you are fulfilling God's call in your life. Genesis 2:18 says, "The LORD God said, 'It is not good for the man to be alone. I will make a helper suitable for him.'"

Isaiah 58:11 tells us, "The LORD will guide you always; he will satisfy your needs in a sun-scorched land." When your future mate fails to meet a need, God is able.

Do you want to serve your future mate? Matthew 7:12 says, "So in everything, do to others what you would have them do to you."

Sometimes you have to set aside your own needs to love another person. Listen to Jesus' command in John 15:12–13: "Love each other as I have loved you. Greater love has no one than this, that he lay down his life for his friends."

Even when you don't feel your needs are being met, remember Philippians 4:19: "My God will meet all your needs according to his glorious riches in Christ Jesus."

5

Keeping It Real

How Do You Communicate Love?

"When we were just getting to know one another, we wanted to be real with each other and get to know each other's hearts," Jennifer says. "So we decided to ask each other three questions, every day, by e-mail. One was a random fun question, but the other two hit the deep places. We tried to be as honest as possible in answering those questions."

"Both of us had already tried the show-only-our-best game when we were dating other people," Ben says, "and we knew that wasn't helpful. So we decided to show the good, the bad, and the ugly up front so we could reveal who we really are. We shared our brokenness, the heartache of our divorces, the choices we'd made, and also what God was doing in us."

It's wise for you to establish positive communication habits early on, like Ben and Jennifer did. Each person enters a relationship with different levels of communication skills and styles, as well as beliefs, thoughts, and fears. But all of us can work on improving our communication with one another.

Susan and I (Dale) worked hard at this early on in our relationship.

We set lots of time aside and talked about our past experiences, our kids, our fears, our concerns. We avoided distractions so we could dig deep and talk openly. And no topic was off-limits, even though some topics weren't easy to discuss. But we knew that if we didn't talk about everything openly and honestly, we'd have surprises that could possibly be hurtful, and we didn't want that.

The hardest part for us was sharing our dreams, because both of us found ourselves lacking the creativity to dream. In the busyness of life, we simply hadn't taken the time or dared to dream. So we started to explore this important area of life, and now we're trying to intentionally live out the dreams we have—like traveling, exploring, and enjoying life to the fullest.

Communication is the lifeblood of any relationship; it will affect every aspect of your marriage. It can help you inform, explain, influence, and build intimacy with each other.

Good personal communication is the act of revealing yourself—your past experiences, present feelings, and future dreams. It's sharing your fears, needs, and desires carefully and honestly. Communicating well is also about setting boundaries, confronting problems, admitting when you're wrong, and extending grace to each other.

"Honesty is paramount," Ben says. "Authenticity—being who we really are, no matter what—is critical. I experienced the lack of it in my first marriage, and I didn't want that again. I'm so glad that Jennifer is the same person whether she's speaking at a conference or sitting on the front porch with me. And I want her to know who I am. I believe that real love is knowing someone with all their faults and loving them still."

When Adam and Eve sinned, they broke the communication they had with their Creator and isolated themselves from Him. They covered up and hid; they were dishonest and ashamed. God never intended that, and He knew that a life of dishonesty and hiding would be painful and counterproductive. That's why God delights in His people overcoming negative communication patterns and learning to communicate in healthy and loving ways.

"Be proactive in revealing who you really are," Ben says. "Learn to be authentic in every area of your life. Allow your mate to know you completely and get to know him or her completely too. And when you're communicating about something, let your mate know what your thought process is, not just the decision you made. Let your partner see how you got there so that he or she can understand how you think and how you make decisions."

Intentional Communication

If we let it, our busy world will hinder the time we have for productive and healthy communication, especially in a blending family with all its complexities. A family's full schedule increases the stress within marriage with its ever-moving, always-busy lifestyle, and then when you add in the kids' schedules, life gets really crazy.

A few years ago, Susan was working sixty-plus hours a week to launch Focus on the Family's *Thriving Family* magazine on time. As founding editor of the publication, she was determined to get everything right, but the stress of the job began to hinder our communication. She came home exhausted, sometimes sick, and she had nothing left for our relationship. I had to be extra patient during this time; she had to be extra aware of the need to keep our communication open and up-to-date. It was a tough season, but we got through it without serious consequences.

In our world today, we have instant communication with cell phones and text messaging. We have constant distractions from the TV, radio, music, people, work, and so on. All this can get in the way of successful communication. And when kids are involved, they sure have a way of distracting and hindering communication, if you're not careful. Between Jennifer and Ben, they have four children. Jennifer has a daughter whom they have primary care for, while Ben has three children—one boy and two girls—who primarily live with their mom, so life is busy.

"Don't let life get in the way of intentionally building your communication and your relationships," Jennifer warns. "Ben and I guard our time together, and this has kept our marriage strong. When one of us isn't traveling, we have our quiet time together and try to do lunch together. Then we have *borreltje* time together—a tradition my parents started when I was little. When Dad got home, he and Mom would spend half an hour together talking and processing the day. It was their private time; no kids were allowed. So we adopted this tradition. We take some time to talk about our day. Both of us take turns talking and listening. Carving out that half hour is so good. And even with little ones, it's possible!"

"Getting past the surface and asking, 'How's your heart?' once in a while is also a good thing," Ben says. "And because of our strong relationship, we feel safe, even when we're direct with each other."

Jennifer and Ben have learned that they have to regularly and intentionally push the pause button, stop, be still, and listen to each other with love, attention, and respect. When we let ourselves get sidetracked by daily life, we tend to take each other for granted. And when outside pressures increase and busyness rules, our closeness decreases and we have the potential for poor communication.

So whatever you choose to call it, we suggest you establish a tradition similar to Ben and Jennifer's *borreltje* time to keep your marriage strong. Find a time that works for you. Susan and I (Dale) try to set aside time to talk and connect before dinner every night.

Loving Communication

In chapter 1 we saw that 1 Corinthians 13:4–8 is our scriptural model for a good marriage relationship: "Love is patient, love is kind. It does not envy, it does not boast, it is not proud. It is not rude, it is not self-seeking, it is not easily angered, it keeps no record of wrongs. Love does not delight in evil but rejoices with the truth. It always protects, always trusts, always hopes, always perseveres. Love never fails."

What's that got to do with communication? Everything! At its best, communication is simply expressing love a thousand different ways—whether it's affirmation, encouragement, being patient and kind, or telling each other we're thankful. It's also admitting when we're wrong and humbly saying we're sorry. Loving communication is sharing thoughts and feelings verbally and nonverbally.

"Because we had such painful experiences in our past relationships," Jennifer says, "I think Ben and I have learned to communicate love in all we say and do. In our previous marriages, we both experienced verbal abuse for many years. So now we have such a sense of gratitude for what we have with each other that we really don't need to worry about the small stuff. A lot of things that may seem important or be irritants to others aren't to us. I know I have this godly man who's kind and good, so why would I be impatient or unkind or pick at the little things? I never want to take this quality companionship for granted."

Susan and I (Dale) can sure relate. So much that used to matter in our earlier years just doesn't matter anymore. In the complexities of remarriage and blending a family, the more you relax and refuse to "sweat the small stuff," the better off you'll be.

Love Is Patient

Patience is one of the most important keys to successful communication. If you want to be loved, respected, trusted, and at peace with yourself, then you'll need to patiently express these attributes to each other. And if your future spouse also shares this vision, you'll be on the road to communicating well.

What does patience in communication look like? It's choosing to demonstrate patience through your attitudes, actions, and verbal interaction, choosing to walk your talk and be real and honest, and allowing the other person to do the same.

"Love covers a multitude of sins," Jennifer says. "Be patient and give each other room not to say everything perfectly or to hear just the right thing. In the midst of trying to communicate, things can come out sideways, or you can look at something from a selfish perspective. As you navigate through each other's quirks and differences, let each other make mistakes, and don't judge your mate if he or she falls short. Give each other grace as you both learn how to communicate well."

Men and women naturally communicate differently—in style, content, emotion, speed, and so on. Dealing with those differences requires a lot of patience. And because the two genders are wired so differently in the ways they think and process information, even more patience is needed! Learning to help your partner understand how and what you are attempting to communicate is often no small task, especially when kids are involved. There are two aspects of communication that affect how you love your future spouse patiently.

1. Communication entails the whole person. It's not just your words that matter. It's your content, the tone of your voice, and the nonverbal signals you send. You communicate with your words, attitude, and actions—these things must work together to send a clear message.

Ben is a salesman. He's a verbal processer, a people person, and an extrovert. Jennifer is a journalistic processer, loves her time alone, and is more of an introvert. Even though their communication styles overlap and generally work well together, communication still takes a lot of effort.

"We're both very affectionate people," Jennifer says, "but Ben is really good at reading my body language. When I try to hide an irritation or something, he can see right through me. And he calls me on it."

"Other times, we can miss or misinterpret those nonverbal signals," Ben says. "Either I won't see it in myself, or I'll miss it in Jennifer. But all of this is so important in communication."

As Ben affirms, in order to have healthy communication, open and honest transparency is necessary. You must walk your talk—your behavior, your facial expressions, and the tone of your voice must match what you say. "You're right" can mean you are mad, sad, happy, afraid, humble, proud—depending on the way you say it and your body language.

Messages can get confusing when you say one thing, but the inflection of your voice and your body signals say another. Statistics say that communication is 38 percent tone, 55 percent body language, and only 7 percent words![1]

"When a situation with his girls is grieving Ben," Jennifer says, "I'll see that it's weighing on him by his body language or other things. He might be quieter or more uptight or less engaged. During moments like that, I try to find a way to defuse the situation and help him through it, whether that means talking about what's going on or sending him off for a hike. Knowing what the other person needs and giving him the freedom to do what he needs to do is important."

"Jennifer's really good about helping me through things that I can't even articulate," Ben says. "I try to find balance to know what I can and can't solve. And I try to let go of the things I can't fix, which is really important in any divorce situation. I do what I can but put the rest in God's care."

Good communication is conveying what is in your heart and knowing that your future spouse lovingly receives it. When you express your thoughts and your partner listens and responds with feedback and understanding, you both become successful communicators and will grow closer in your relationship.

2. Men and women are different. As you know, most women love to talk. You also know that most women speak mainly from their emotions, while men often speak mainly from logic. Men often find it harder to articulate things than women. No wonder we need patience with each other! But we can learn how to work with each other's different communication styles.

"When Jennifer's daughter, Beth, tries to manipulate her mom," Ben says, "I make sure that I support Jennifer and let her process through it, even though the male in me wants to just fix it and tell her what to do. Sometimes I give her suggestions to either balance her or give her options, but patience is letting her work through it, and kindness is letting her process things without always giving her my opinion. This is actually the best way to help and support her."

While men have often been taught that showing their feelings is a sign of weakness or unmanliness, Ben has learned how to be transparent and open with Jennifer. God gave each of us feelings for a reason, and He communicates His feelings of love, anger, concern, tenderness, loyalty, and much more to us. Since we are created in His likeness, He expects all of us to express our thoughts and emotions as we relate to others. I (Susan) was so glad that Dale's mom taught him this early on, and I'm sure his two master's degrees in counseling reinforced this as well. It certainly has made our communication a lot easier!

Men may have to leave their comfort zone of quiet contemplation and painfully express their feelings, fears, and emotions. Women may have to leave their comfort zone of saying anything they want, when they want, and learn to be sensitive to their man. It's part of the journey we all need to make to become mature and effective communicators.

"It's more important for me to know what Jennifer is feeling than to agree with those feelings," Ben says. "To me, that's loving communication. Knowing her heart, I know she has what's best for us in mind. Even if we disagree on something, we feel safe to share on a deep and real level. We don't have to be perfect, and we don't always have to have the same interests. But we can trust each other."

Love Is Kind

Successful communication is also about being kind and considerate of each other, and that comes when there's a balance between speaking and listening. Loving communication is a two-sided coin. On one side is using kind words; on the other is employing considerate listening.

1. Kind words create intimacy. We should choose to use kind words to affirm, praise, support, give feedback, paint word pictures, brainstorm, share details of an event, write notes, and love our future mates and their children. These are only a few ways to create intimate communication. But every one of these takes a conscious choice to communicate with kindness.

"Communicating with kindness is so important," Jennifer says. "In the early years of our marriage, we dealt with a lot of difficult things; our exes for starters, and then Ben's son Jeff, who struggles with bipolar disorder, moving in with us were a couple of the toughest difficulties. At that time, my young teen daughter had all the issues that puberty and life change bring. We moved across country. Then we had major health problems and surgeries, a car accident, and job changes. Dealing with other people's anger, mental instability, revenge, and more—we just had to be open, honest, and work as a team to overcome these challenges. And we had to communicate with extra measures of kindness."

To fill up their love bank during those stressful times, Jennifer and Ben took special times alone as a couple. "We had to withdraw from the chaos and spend time together," Jennifer said. "Giving words of affirmation and encouragement was huge. Touch was very important. When there are a lot of stress and high-conflict situations in your life, it's so important to affirm the other person. Ben would take time to say thank you for how I handled a situation, even if I did it 90 percent wrong! He found a way to pull out the nugget of what I did do right."

As Ben and Jennifer found out, even when you're in the midst of a stressful situation—or angry as a hornet—you can still maintain the right heart attitude as you convey information, discuss difficult topics, and even vent. You can show your respect, support, and love by consciously choosing your words and speaking with a kind and loving attitude. Yes, it takes diligence and restraint, but if you choose to be careful about what you say and how you say it, you can succeed, even in the toughest situation.

Kind communication is also other-centered and honest. Using "I" statements instead of the accusatory "You" statements is a simple way to communicate well. Instead of saying "You never clean the counter," you can say, "I feel unappreciated when I have to always clean the kitchen counter." It's a simple twist with a big reward. The listener feels empathy for you instead of feeling accused by you.

For both Dale and me (Susan), this type of communication takes a conscious effort, since we didn't learn it growing up. We have to choose to be careful about what we say, and we try to avoid saying things that will hurt the other person. Though there are times when one of us says something that irritates the other, we try to assess whether we really need to address it or need to let it go. Our motto is "If we can't say something nice, just don't say it!"

2. Considerate listening creates intimacy. Intentionally listening to some-one shows that you love and care about him or her. It takes concentration, acceptance, empathy, and choosing to care enough to hear what's behind the words. When you hear your future mate's heart, understand his or her message, and accept each other with all your shortcomings, you create a place of safety, a place to build and mature as individuals and as a couple.

"Sometimes Jennifer has to call me out on my lack of listening skills," Ben admits. "It's easy to give her my full attention when I'm with her, be-cause I see her face-to-face. But when I'm traveling and we're talking on the phone, I'll get busy multitasking, so I might be answering an e-mail while trying to listen to her. Not good. I'm learning how important it is to have focused time with each other, either on the phone or face-to-face. I love her, and I know that's an important part of communicating well."

Many of us have never really learned to listen well. We've learned to be selective listeners—sifting information, ignoring details, and allowing ourselves to be distracted by everything around us. In today's media-driven world, we're often living on information overload. We have concerns at work, at home, with the kids, with friends, in our communities, in our nation, and around the world. That breeds distraction, and we have to proactively be careful not to allow the cares of the world to break down our relationships; we have to choose to listen carefully to those we love.

To listen well, you have to be considerate of the other person's need to communicate with you. That means you have to choose to shut out the distractions around you and engage with that person with your whole being—your eyes, ears, and heart. You need to give him or her your undivided attention. Sometimes just shutting off the music or muting the television shows interest and respect for the other person and contributes to good communication. Other times, it might take going for a walk together or a drive to get away from the distractions of home.

The truth is, Dale and I (Susan) still struggle with this. We might be in separate rooms or even on separate floors, but we somehow think that one of us will magically tune in to what the other is saying. Over time we've begun to recognize moments that are best suited to talking and sharing and moments that aren't. We've learned that when we're driving in traffic, it's hard for us to concentrate on a deep discussion.

Dale knows that when I'm in my writing mode and on the computer, it's hard for me to listen well or try to have a discussion. We laugh about it. We try to do better. But the reality is that we're still working on improving our listening skills and changing our tendency to try to communicate when one of us is busy or distracted.

Your objective is to find the right time to talk with your future spouse and then find out what he or she is really trying to say. It helps if once you've listened to your partner, you then verify that what he or she actually said is really what you heard.

Though Ben and Jennifer have learned these skills, they have to be continually intentional in communicating with each other because they know that good communication takes a lifetime.

🌱 BLENDING WITH KIDS

How Can We Communicate Well with Our Children and Stepchildren?

The challenges of communicating well in a blending family are many. Past hurts, current perceptions, expectations, and fears or frustrations affect our ability to communicate well. The adjustment process is a long and winding road, so extra measures of patience and kindness help when communicating with kids and stepkids.

"Jennifer's daughter, Beth, was twelve when her mom and I met," Ben says, "so in the beginning, Jennifer was the parent 100 percent of the time. I was an acquaintance to Beth and let her set the pace for her relationship with me. I let her develop a trust in me as she got to know me; I never wanted her to feel vulnerable or fearful around me. Jennifer and I agreed that she would do all the disciplining with Beth, so I simply gave Beth my love and encouragement. Today, I'll give her advice, and sometimes I have to intervene and support my wife, but I still don't take on the discipline and authority role."

"We are really cautious about what we say about one another's kids," Jennifer admits. "Ben knows that comments about Beth will be more sensitive for me, so he's careful about measuring his words, adding in affirmation, and not judging her or me."

"There's a vulnerability in a remarriage situation that's unique," Ben says. "If you're both the biological parents, you can rail about your kids all night long. You can be very raw and real. But in remarriage, there's more ownership of the biological child's words and actions, so the biological parent can take comments more personally. You have to be very sensitive of those bonds."

Susan and I (Dale) strongly agree with this. We've found it to be true for us as we discuss our adult children and even our grandchildren. Be careful in all you say and do regarding each other's kids—after all, they are a part of the one you love.

"The biological parent always has the final say," Jennifer says. "We may choose to do something differently with our own kids than with our stepkids, but we know our own kids better. So each of us needs to honor and yield to the choices our spouse makes. We need to respect his or her decisions and support our spouse."

A year after they married, Ben's twenty-one-year-old son, Jeff, moved in with them, and there were times that the sparks would fly between Beth and Jeff. "Ben and I had to be sure we were united," Jennifer says. "We had to present a united front, or it'd be easy to divide into biological camps. Those were very difficult times. Jeff was highly emotional, sometimes irrational, and Ben would push back. But in all of the conflict, Ben and I had to withdraw to a private place and figure out how to work through it. We were so dependent on God and each other during those times."

"As the man of the house, I needed to set the tone," Ben says. "We wanted a house of peace and safety, and I had to enforce that. We couldn't tolerate the outbursts and the fits. There were more than a few times that I had to ask Jeff to leave the house."

"I'm so glad Ben set that boundary," Jennifer says. "And I was so thankful that he guarded our home and kept it a safe place."

"Jennifer and I have the same values, and we want the same outcome," Ben says. "We love God and know that He's our hope. We couldn't let our values be compromised, and we had to enforce them in our home. And I made sure I spoke highly of Jennifer when talking with Jeff. It's important that the kids know how much we appreciate our spouse and how much our spouse cares for them. Sometimes it just needs to be brought to their attention."

The complex nature of communicating well in a blending family is obvious. But with love and understanding, it can be done.

❧ APPRAISING MY LIFE

Now it's time to assess your level of patience and kindness in communication. Identify one area where you need to improve your communication.

Watching your tone of voice? Monitoring your body language? Being honest and transparent? Measuring your words? Making yourself articulate your thoughts?

Discuss your assessment with your future mate, asking him or her to patiently and kindly help you improve in this area of communication. For more ways to do this, we suggest that you read *Love and Respect* by Emerson Eggerichs. This book will help you learn how to really love your wife and respect your husband.

✿ ASSESSING OUR LIVES

How would you rate yourselves as a couple on how well you show patience for each other? Name three areas in which you need your future mate to exhibit more patience. In talking over tough issues? In planning your wedding? In discussing the kids? In making future plans together? In reading this book?

Discuss these three areas and pray together, asking God to help you grow. Then decide from the following list which communication-building traditions you'd like to establish in your marriage.

- Morning and evening chats: Start and end your day with a few minutes of uninterrupted time together.
- Home-from-work transition time: When one or both of you get home from work, take a few minutes to reconnect. Never be "too busy."
- Kiss-'n'-hug: Don't go a day without a heartfelt kiss and hug. It may sound silly now, but later in your marriage, it'll be a tradition you'll be grateful you established.
- Mealtimes: Pray over each meal, holding hands. We started the tradition of giving each other a quick kiss after we pray; kids might think it's sappy, but showing affection is a good example for them.

- Dates: Never lose the romance. Go on dates regularly, and guys, if she says she needs a date, listen to her!
- Prayer time: Establish daily prayer time together.
- Decision time: When decisions need to be made or concerns need to be aired, set aside a specific time to do so. (We'll talk more about this in chapter 6.)

🌱 A MOMENT FOR FUN!

What one object would best show your personality?

Imagine you could own only one book (not the Bible). What would you choose and why?

🌱 APPLYING GOD'S WORD

Following are some scriptures on patience and kindness. Read them together as a couple; then choose one scripture that can help you grow in the area of loving communication. Memorize the verse together.

An anxious heart weighs a man down, but a kind word cheers him up. (Proverbs 12:25)

A patient man has great understanding, but a quick-tempered man displays folly. (Proverbs 14:29)

A hot-tempered man stirs up dissension, but a patient man calms a quarrel. (Proverbs 15:18)

Better a patient man than a warrior, a man who controls his temper than one who takes a city. (Proverbs 16:32)

Love your enemies, do good to them, and lend to them without expecting to get anything back. Then your reward will be great, and you will be sons of the Most High, because he is kind to the ungrateful and wicked. (Luke 6:35)

Be joyful in hope, patient in affliction, faithful in prayer. (Romans 12:12)

Be completely humble and gentle; be patient, bearing with one another in love. (Ephesians 4:2)

Be kind and compassionate to one another, forgiving each other, just as in Christ God forgave you. (Ephesians 4:32)

And we urge you, brothers, warn those who are idle, encourage the timid, help the weak, be patient with everyone. (1 Thessalonians 5:14)

Make sure that nobody pays back wrong for wrong, but always try to be kind to each other and to everyone else. (1 Thessalonians 5:15)

[Women are] to be self-controlled and pure, to be busy at home, to be kind, and to be subject to their husbands, so that no one will malign the word of God. (Titus 2:5)

Be patient, then, brothers, until the Lord's coming. See how the farmer waits for the land to yield its valuable crop and how patient he is for the autumn and spring rains. (James 5:7)

6

Clearing the Air

How Can You Resolve Conflict Well?

$\mathcal{L}$ ess than a year into Gayle and Steve's second marriage, Gayle's ex-husband was arrested and jailed for murder! A horrifying trial ensued, and the children suffered extreme emotional trauma. The life sentence without parole meant that Gayle's kids no longer had their father in their lives. On top of the stress of the trial, Gayle and Steve both worked stressful jobs as well as juggled the everyday challenges of blending a family, and it's safe to say that conflict was common—and resolving those conflicts required love, commitment, and so much more.

Just ask any second-marriage couple if conflict is more likely to happen in a blended family, and they'll all say, "Of course!" Resolving conflict is a challenge under the best of circumstances, but in Gayle and Steve's case, the external stress seemed to be on steroids! Even so, their determination to resolve conflict together has enabled this couple's relationship to be a shining example of a strong second marriage.

Conflict can happen for lots of reasons: when your self-esteem is threatened, when you feel mistreated or misunderstood, when you feel you've been treated unjustly or unfairly, or even when one of you is just in a bad mood. Though every couple will deal with disagreements, in a second marriage you often add conflict with—or over—the children into the mix. Some of the conflict may stem from the residue of a prior marriage, from the pain of a divorce or a death, or from the children not accepting your relationship. Add to that some kind of unexpected trauma, whether external or internal, and you have a perfect storm.

But it's not impossible to navigate through even the most difficult times. Resolving conflict is a skill that can be acquired. Yes, it requires maturity, a positive attitude, a willingness to be open and honest, and lots of flexibility. Most of all, it requires determination and reliance on God's help. But it can be done, and your marriage can be stronger for it.

Our circumstances weren't nearly as dramatic as Steve and Gayle's, but they were challenging nonetheless. Susan's adult son came to visit us three months after we were married, and that visit turned into a nine-month stay. Although Susan dearly loved her son, he had some negative traits that, all too often, brought her to tears. Amid these challenges, I (Dale) had two major surgeries, and the stress of it all caused us to call on God to help us through the conflicts that arose that first year.

Starting Out Well

As we discussed in chapter 2, making sure you're ready to remarry is so important, and assessing what you've learned through the journey of resolving conflict in your prior relationships will help you be successful moving forward.

"You absolutely have to do your homework and know what went wrong in the first marriage so that you won't repeat the past," Gayle says. "It's too easy to point the finger and say it was all your ex-spouse's fault. But you had a part in it too, so what do you need to learn from that experience? Were your reactions wrong? Did you stuff your emotions? Or did you simply not know how to resolve conflict? Fortunately, Steve and I took the time to figure those things out, so we rarely repeat the same mistakes we used to make. If we hadn't, the stress of the trial might have been too much to handle."

"But we still have things to learn," Steve says with a smile. "I learned early in my marriage to Gayle that you never use name-calling as a weapon!"

"Steve is very close to the Lord and follows Him, and that makes all the difference," Gayle says. "When I mess up, Steve quickly forgives, lets it all go, and moves on. Forgiveness is very important in keeping things right between us."

"But it's a journey," Steve adds. "Lately, I've had to correct a pattern of murmuring—muttering under my breath when I don't like something Gayle's son, Jack, does. It hurts Gayle, and it's wrong. So I've asked God to help me with that."

Indeed, none of us will ever be perfect, but we can continually work on our own issues. And with God's help, our behavior patterns will improve.

What Really Matters

Picking and choosing your battles is very important in any marriage, but it's critical in a second marriage. There are simply too many things going on, and if you constantly nitpick, you'll create an atmosphere of ongoing conflict.

"The second time around," Gayle says, "you realize that so much of the stuff that seemed so big when you were younger isn't really that big after all. In reality, about 20 percent of the time, we do have those spontaneous combustible moments and don't deal with things well. But thankfully, about 80 percent of the time, we do it well. Most of all, we have learned to be careful in how we deal with any kind of conflict, especially when it comes to disagreements about the kids."

Assessing your situation and responding accordingly will help you prioritize what really matters. When blending a family, many couples find creative ways to make peace in the midst of seeming chaos.

"When we got married, Gayle was simply exhausted," Steve says. "She was a single working mom of four kids, and that was tough. Then within a year we had the massive stress of a trial and the kids testifying. Emotionally, we were spent. We still had to keep working at our jobs. We had to make life happen. And even though there were things that could have caused disagreements, they just weren't worth fighting over. We had to go into survival mode. Because we'd experienced the conflict of going through nasty divorces and all that comes with that, we had already learned to let a lot of stuff go. But best of all, I've always been sure of Gayle's love for me, and if I need to bring something up, I know she'll work with me to resolve it."

Even though Gayle and Steve's situation seems extreme, many couples face similar challenges, minus a murder trial. There's too much to do, and there's not enough time and energy. But couples can still be successful in the midst of it all. And even when you experience those "combustible" moments, God's grace and forgiveness are available to you.

Gayle and Steve learned to dance the beautiful dance of picking their battles, learning from mistakes, saying "I'm sorry," forgiving each other, and moving on. Because of that, their marriage is continually growing and being strengthened, even through all the bumps—and sometimes the land mines—along their second-marriage road.

The Ex Files

When you lose a spouse through death, the grieving process can be all-consuming; however, you aren't faced with the ongoing complexities of interactions with an ex-spouse. In a divorce, the ex, the father or mother of our children, is most often an ever-present reality, and that can cause conflict.

"We discovered early on that our times of conflict seemed to regularly revolve around our exes," Steve says. "Otherwise, we simply didn't have a lot of conflict. But when one of the ex-spouses fired one of us up, we'd get the other fired up, and then it could spiral out of control. We finally got so tired of talking about our exes that we decided to set aside and limit a time to talk only about the ex issues. Then, when we were done, we were done."

"If we didn't do that, it would get control of us," Gayle says. "We had to take control of the external factors that were affecting our marriage. When you're talking about your exes or your kids, it can get dicey. That can end up taking a lot of your time, emotions, and energy, and before you know it, you have nothing left for each other."

"There are always the normal stressors of second marriages and blended families—custody issues, child support, visitation, and that kind of thing," Steve says. "And though you're not really arguing with each other, the stress is there. You have to manage that stress so it doesn't affect your relationship."

"What we didn't know initially," Gayle says, "is that it's very easy to revert back to your old patterns of conflict resolution. We had to realize this, make a conscious effort to change those old patterns, and find healthy ones that worked. For us, making appointments to discuss those things worked well."

Dale and I (Susan) suggest that you take some time to reflect on your previous conflict-resolution patterns and learn from them. Dale and I were naturally nonconfrontational, so avoidance was our primary pattern of dealing with conflict. That wasn't good either. So we consciously have to step out of our comfort zones to attempt to resolve conflict rather than avoid it.

Knowing how you're wired will help you push through to a healthy method of conflict resolution.

Fight or Flight

All of us tend to have a certain way of resolving conflict—one of four basic fighting styles:

1. I'll win at all costs (we control and attack).
2. I'll never win (we give up).
3. I'll withdraw (we just let it go or ignore it).
4. We'll work together to resolve the issue.

Though Gayle and Steve's default mode was to win at all costs, they learned to change their style so they could resolve the issues they faced as a team.

"Both of us are competitive by nature," Gayle says. "Unfortunately, that means we both have that 'I *will* win' mentality. So we have to choose to work together. Though it may be our tendency, we no longer jump into fights anymore. It usually starts with a discussion and maybe gets a little heated. So we may wait to discuss the issue later if we need to. But we never avoid a problem like we both did in our first marriages. We have learned—the hard way—that avoiding a problem is *not* the answer. If we don't have the energy to talk about it right then, we table it for a day or so and think it through."

"We probably table our discussions about 80 percent of the time," Steve says, "because too often there's something competing for our time— work, a sporting event with one of the boys, whatever. The next day we schedule a time to resolve the issue."

As in any conflict, resolving an issue takes a concerted effort. Gayle and Steve had to find out how to do that in their circumstances, and so will you.

Here are some basics. First, check your attitude, making sure that self- ishness, anger, or stubbornness isn't controlling you. Then ask for God's help, especially when dealing with touchy subjects such as sex, money, or the kids. Next, take ownership of your emotions and reactions and analyze the problem to find out if it is, in fact, the actual problem. What's really going on? Like Gayle and Steve, be sure it's the right time to talk about the situation, and never argue in public or in front of the kids, especially about something as personal as sex or kid stuff.

After all this, you're ready to discuss the problem. Be sure to use "I" statements instead of pointing the finger and blaming your partner, as Steve learned. Don't use name-calling, lash out with explosive words, or push each other's buttons while you're trying to resolve an issue.

Here's the bottom line: Treat one another the way you'd want to be treated! Listen to each other, find a solution together, forgive one another, and resolve to learn from the experience. Then celebrate overcoming conflict yet again—together.

Take a Break

At times things can get really heated when couples are in the middle of resolving a conflict. Gayle and Steve have realized that during those times, they simply need to take a break from the discussion.

"There are times when it gets so stressful that we just need our space to calm down, regroup, and take some alone time," Steve says. "We have learned to compartmentalize things, to let things sit, to go to work and do our jobs well, to process the problem, and then deal with it when we're able to do it justice."

"We've also learned not to demand that things get resolved immediately," Gayle says. "We give each other the space to process. The caveat is that we also need to reassure one another that it's okay, that each of us is safe in this marriage. Once we are reassured of each other's love, Steve takes 'garage time,' while I might wander around the mall or go out for coffee. It gives us time to think things through without the pressure of having to figure things out right then and there."

"As long as I know that I'm personally not the problem, I'm okay," Steve says. "And I reassure Gayle that she's not the problem and that I will always be there. If I retreat to the garage, she knows that I'll be back, that I'll reengage, and that we'll solve the problem together. We do this so that the wounds of the past can't haunt us or cloud our thinking. That way we can relax and process things well. Often we also need the time alone with God so He can help."

Keep in mind that when you're dealing with conflict, sometimes taking a break to calm down and regroup can be very beneficial. In the next four sections, we'll take a look at some of those hot-button topics that can often become sources of conflict, and we'll gain some perspective by learning how Gayle and Steve worked through them.

Money

We all know that finances can be a hot-button issue, especially in these uncertain economic times. (We'll discuss this more in chapter 8.) So can issues of safety, values, honesty, trust, or any number of other things. But in a second marriage particularly, money issues are often a reality that can cause lots of conflict. Fortunately, by being proactive about this important issue, you can avoid conflicts that result from opposing views or differing expectations.

"Though finances can bring stress," Steve says, "they don't have to rule your relationship. Before we got married, we learned everything possible about each other's finances. There was nothing hidden. There were no surprises. We paid down all of Gayle's debt, and we knew we had to plan carefully and figure out how to live within our means."

"We have separate as well as combined bank accounts, but we also have a joint family budget," Gayle says. "We know what expenses come out of Steve's paycheck and what come out of mine, and we figure out our finances together. I'm the intentional saver, so when we have unexpected expenses, it's stressful for me, and that's a recipe for conflict. But Steve understands my needs, and we figure out the problem together. That helps us avoid a lot of conflict over money."

"The kids' expenses also affect us," Steve says, "but we rarely argue over it. We just deal with it."

"Child support is a real frustration," Gayle admits, "because I feel like I have to work full-time to support Steve's ex so she can stay home. When she and her second husband took Steve to court to get more of his paycheck, that was a tough one. Though things like this cause short-term conflict between us, we realize that it is what it is, and we refuse to let our marriage suffer because of outside forces."

Though finances can often cause a lot of conflict, Steve and Gayle have learned how to resolve their financial challenges by keeping things in a healthy perspective.

Sex

Sex is another hot topic that can cause conflict. (We'll address this more deeply in chapter 9). The basic differences between men and women physically, mentally, and emotionally naturally affect a marital relationship. In a second marriage (or third or fourth), factors such as extra stress, the presence of children in the home, or past relationships and experiences can also incite disagreements, frustrations, or other tensions about sex.

"Early on, sex is often great," Gayle says. "But the stresses of family life and work can easily get the best of you. As you get older, physical changes can also take a toll. Sometimes intimacy takes a hit, and that can bring conflict. For a woman, there are also the issues of body image, emotions, and hormones on top of exhaustion. In my situation, Steve has been wonderfully understanding and patient."

"I simply had to deal with my own selfishness," Steve says. "When there's so much stress, it affects intimacy. I just won't let the circumstances bring conflict into this area of my marriage."

"We came to a place of needing to sit down and discuss these challenges," Gayle says. "We discussed our needs, and though that was hard to work through, we resolved the issues."

"What does sexual intimacy look like?" Steve asks. "What it looked like when we were in our twenties without kids was very different from what it looks like now. You have to be okay with that. You have to be willing to talk about it, to be open and honest and vulnerable."

"For some second-marriage couples, the baggage from the first marriage also makes things more difficult," Gayle says. "Because of scars from the past, I needed to feel safe, and Steve helps me feel that in our relationship. As long as you communicate and agree together, there doesn't have to be that added tension, and certainly not ongoing conflict."

If you're still struggling with sexual issues, scars, or hurts from the past, be sure to get some help (talk with your pastor or a counselor) and resolve them before you marry. Otherwise, these issues will likely affect your relationship. And if you find that sexual intimacy becomes a place of conflict after you marry, remember to resolve it like Steve and Gayle did—they were gentle and vulnerable as they talked, and they were understanding in the midst of challenging circumstances.

Time Conflicts

Second-marriage couples tend to get so busy running the kids here and there that they let their private couple time fall by the wayside. But that's not healthy for your marriage.

"We have to be intentional about making time together," Gayle says. "But instead of expecting a certain amount of couple time, we have to be creative and find time together when we can. Sometimes it's a lunch or when the boys are sleeping or at sports practice, but we find the time to be together. Because life is so busy, we have to let couple time happen when we can."

"One of my favorite times," Steve says, "is when just the two of us go to a restaurant at nine o'clock at night and share an appetizer. That's just how it is in this season of life."

Gayle says, "We also need to make time to get away as a couple. It's different for every couple, but for us, a yearly vacation is best. Whether it's a weekly date night, a once-a-month getaway, a quarterly weekend away, or a longer yearly vacation, we know we have to do something and take that time to wind down, destress, spend quality time together, and reconnect."

Gayle and Steve learned to reduce their conflicts over time together by adjusting their expectations for this season of their lives. Yet they were also proactive in finding time together when they could. In a blending family, this is a critical thing to do.

The Kid Factor

Perhaps the most challenging aspect of a second marriage is the kid factor. Though we know that every one of our children is a gift from God, they do add stress, and often, conflict.

"There's always been a parenting rub," Gayle says. "Being a single mother with four kids, I had to be a more strict parent than Steve is with his son. And because our parenting styles are different, I don't feel that I can parent my youngest son, Jack, like I did my three older kids, so that's been tough for me. In a blended family, you have to figure out how to make it all work, not only for you as a couple, but also for the kids."

"The differences in how we parent caused a lot of conflict early on," Steve says. "The two boys were eight and nine when we married. Our biggest conflicts were in raising them—each of us having a biological son—and the boys sure weren't the best of friends."

"My three older children were in and out of the home," Gayle says. "They were busy with college and young-adult stuff, so they didn't affect us too much. But the two boys were a different story. Each of the boys carried his own emotional baggage. They were just a year apart in school, they had very different personalities, and they had a lot of rivalry, especially in sports."

"So when conflict pulled the boys apart, it began to pull Gayle and me apart," Steve says. "We had to learn to not let their stuff affect us so much."

This is a learning process for most second-marriage couples. When multiple stepsiblings are in the home, things can get complicated, and it takes even more care.

"What ended up happening was that I disciplined my son, and Steve disciplined his," Gayle said. "But because I was more strict, I was usually the bad guy. Jack felt it was unjust, and it seemed so unfair to him."

"The whole parenting thing was extra hard because within a year of my joining the family, Jack's dad went to jail for life," Steve adds. "So I ended up stepping in as a full-time dad to Jack. Life with Jack hasn't been a smooth road, but I love him and I'm doing my best to be the father figure he needs."

"I realize that Steve's son, Kevin, already has a full-time mom," Gayle says, "so I don't need to take the lead with him. And even when I do need to speak to Kevin about something, it's different from how I handle things with Jack. It isn't easy, but that's life in a blending family."

"The older kids naturally don't like it when Gayle and I are at odds," Steve says. "We've tried to keep our conflicts from them as much as possible, but they see them. They sense a disagreement, and they have their opinions. But Gayle and I have to settle things, just the two of us, regardless of what others think."

"Steve's presence is such a blessing, such a stabilizing force in our family," Gayle says. "I don't know that I could've handled the trial and the jail stuff on my own, and God knew that. We've been through so much that the only things we have conflicts over now are really serious issues. Those nitpicky things—like critiquing the way the other person drives or how he or she does laundry—just don't matter. They aren't worth fighting over."

"It's not always rosy," says Steve, "but things could sure be worse! To be honest, in some ways we've actually been through worse stuff in this marriage than we experienced in our first marriages. But we've chosen to take the high road in the midst of it all. The D word is not an option. Each day is a choice to work through whatever we need to. When all is said and done, I want to have my stepkids at my funeral saying, 'He loved our mom.' I want to be the husband and father that my family needs me to be."

"Our marriage is good, and our families are blending," Gayle says. "And for better or worse, we *are* a family!"

☙ BLENDING WITH KIDS

How Can Stepparents Resolve Conflicts with Stepchildren?
Resolving stepparent-stepchild conflict is definitely a delicate dance. Knowing your role will help you both avoid and resolve conflicts that may arise with your stepchildren. Whether it's conflict over loyalty, resentment, confusion, time demands, duties, or whatever, knowing how to proceed will help you be successful. Though Gayle and Steve's roles ended up very different, the fact is, they found their way through those tough stepparenting issues.

Because stepparents earn authority by building relationship, effective stepparents *gradually* move into disciplinary roles. In *The Smart Stepfamily*, Ron Deal provides wise advice for successful stepparenting. He describes three positive relationship styles that establish parental authority and help empower you to resolve conflicts that may come your way:[1]

1. The "babysitter" role: Babysitters have power to manage children only if the parents give them power. Biological parents must pass power to stepparents shortly after remarriage so that children will understand that stepparents are not acting on their own authority.

2. The "uncle/aunt" role: After a solid foundation for a relationship has developed, stepparents can move into the "uncle or

aunt" stepparenting role. Stepparents can become more authoritative, clearly communicating limits and encouraging discussion of family rules.

3. The "parent" or stepparent role: Eventually, some stepparents will gain "parental" status with their stepchildren. Younger children tend to grant stepparent status much more quickly than adolescents. It is quite common to be considered a babysitter by an older child, an aunt by a middle child, and a parent by the youngest child. It is important that stepparents not consider themselves failures if they don't achieve parental status with every child. Enjoy the relationship you have now, and trust the integration process.

✿ APPRAISING MY LIFE

How did you handle conflict in your first marriage? What did you do right? What did you do wrong? What will you change in your second marriage?

✿ ASSESSING OUR LIVES

What has caused conflict between the two of you thus far? Were they misunderstandings? Unrealized expectations? Unmet needs? Annoying habits? Your kids? Your former spouses? Talk about your hot buttons together and make a plan to deal with them well.

Between the two of you, how much conflict revolves around the kids? What causes the most conflict? The kids vying for your time or attention? Jealousy? Rivalry? What can you do as a couple to help your children in these areas? Brainstorm ways to alleviate some of these conflicts before you marry.

✼ A MOMENT FOR FUN!

What was your favorite college course and why?

Imagine you could relive a moment of your childhood. What would it be?

✼ APPLYING GOD'S WORD

If we believe the Bible is the owner's manual for our lives, then we believe that within it there is wisdom for every problem. Following God's Word is the best way to resolve conflict.

Here are ten steps to resolving conflict and guidance from God's Word on each issue:

1. *Attitude:* Prepare your heart. Ephesians 4:31–32 says, "Get rid of all bitterness, rage and anger, brawling and slander, along with every form of malice. Be kind and compassionate to one another, forgiving each other, just as in Christ God forgave you."

2. *Ask:* Seek God's help. James 3:17–18 says, "But the wisdom that comes from heaven is first of all pure; then peace-loving, considerate, submissive, full of mercy and good fruit, impartial and sincere. Peacemakers who sow in peace raise a harvest of righteousness."

3. *Assume:* Own your feelings. Proverbs 28:13 says, "He who conceals his sins does not prosper, but whoever confesses and renounces them finds mercy."

4. *Analyze:* Define the problem. James 4:1 says, "What causes fights and quarrels among you? Don't they come from your desires that battle within you?"

5. *Atmosphere:* Make a loving atmosphere a priority. First Peter 4:8 says, "Above all, love each other deeply, because love covers over a multitude of sins."

6. *Articulate:* Speak the truth in love. Ephesians 4:15 says, "Instead, speaking the truth in love, we will in all things grow up into him who is the Head, that is, Christ."

7. *Assess:* Listen and respond. Proverbs 20:3 says, "It is to a man's honor to avoid strife, but every fool is quick to quarrel."

8. *Agree:* Agree on a solution. Proverbs 12:15 says, "The way of a fool seems right to him, but a wise man listens to advice."

9. *Answer:* Resolve and forgive. Colossians 3:12–14 says, "Therefore, as God's chosen people, holy and dearly loved, clothe yourselves with compassion, kindness, humility, gentleness and patience. Bear with each other and forgive whatever grievances you may have against one another. Forgive as the Lord forgave

you. And over all these virtues put on love, which binds them all together in perfect unity."

10. *Applaud:* Move on in victory. Philippians 4:8 says, "Finally, brothers, whatever is true, whatever is noble, whatever is right, whatever is pure, whatever is lovely, whatever is admirable—if anything is excellent or praiseworthy—think about such things."

7

Dynamic Differences

Can Our Differences Be Gifts from God?

*E*very couple in this book has told us how they marvel at the wonder of truly being loved by another person—despite their differences, quirks, habits, and other foibles that can disrupt an ordinary person's world. For us, it's no different. Dale and I (Susan) have fifteen years between us, so I was a toddler while he was in high school! We raised our children differently—his kids were raised in a secular environment, while mine went to a Christian school and were raised in the church. He was in the military; I worked in Christian ministry. So our different backgrounds could have been a challenge, but we've made them assets. We've learned so much through each other, have helped others because of our differences, and have grown closer through it all. You can too.

Though differences are real and are a part of daily life, they don't have to impact your life together in a detrimental way—if you keep the proper perspective! That's a beautiful part of the remarriage adventure.

"I think it's an amazing thing to learn to love someone so different," Megan says. "This second marriage makes me appreciate the unique and different ways God makes us. I respect Tom so much, even with his quirks."

"It's a great thing to know that this marriage is something God put together," Tom says. "We can laugh at our differences and the things that don't really matter."

"The things that used to annoy me in my former marriage really don't matter anymore," Megan admits. "I'm not out to change Tom. I'm just so grateful that I have someone who's so good to me and loves me and who's a good-willed man. When you've been hurt so badly in your first marriage and then you're treated well in your second, all those differences are tiny, unimportant details in the grand scheme of things."

Tom and Megan are right; so much is about perspective. Some differences probably attracted you to each other initially, but when you live with them 24/7, they can also be frustrating, confusing, exasperating, and unnerving, if you let them be. Dealing with differences well is about attitude.

"When we went to the premarital classes, we told everyone we had no differences and were very much alike," Tom says. "Everyone laughed when we said we'd never had a fight and didn't think we ever would. Later we found that because we are so much alike, we tend to step on each other's toes!"

"It took us a long time to figure out that our similar personalities actually caused us to get on each other's nerves," Megan admits. "We both are doers and think our way is the best way. So when one of us does something differently from how the other thinks it should be done, it's hard for the other to adjust."

"I still struggle with discussing things with Megan instead of just doing something on my own," Tom says. "But I do realize that my way isn't always the only—or the best—way. You may think being so similar is an asset, but be careful. When both of you are decision makers and doers, it's hard to let go of what you're used to, and you can easily frustrate each other."

"And even if you think your way is better, step back, and let the other person do it the way he or she is used to," Megan warns. "You can avoid do-overs by respecting each other's choices."

Like Tom and Megan, managing differences can be a delicate balancing act. Sometimes we get myopic—seeing our way of doing things as the only right way. We have to adjust our thinking to see that differences aren't wrong, they are just different; and they can actually help us remain humble and unselfish as we grow, stretch, and mature as individuals.

"When we married, I moved into Tom's house," Megan says, "and it wasn't easy for him to let me be a part of making the renovation decisions and changing the house. It was also hard for me to move into his home. But we worked through it together, even when we differed on what we wanted to do."

"It was financially a better decision to keep my house and renovate it," Tom says, "but I would encourage couples to get a place of their own if they can, especially if the kids lived in the other home."

"Since Tom's kids lived in his home, when we were renovating, they had a hard time with the changes too," Megan says. "We were changing *their* home. They had expectations of having a Christmas tree in a certain place and stuff like that, so it was more troubling for them than it was for my kids."

Negotiating differences isn't easy. Whether differences stem from your genders or personalities, or from your past histories, it's important to know how they may affect your relationship. But God can use those differences to make you better people.

Dealing with Differences

God's plan for your marriage is to transform you as individuals, and then for you to balance each other through the differences each of you brings to the marriage. When you work with your differences (instead of against them), you not only mature into stronger Christians, but you can also help each other heal and grow through your past hurts and mistakes.

"The fact that I can trust Tom is so refreshing," Megan says. "In my former marriage, I was lied to frequently. I continue to feel such healing in knowing that Tom is trustworthy. To have a relationship in which I can believe my spouse is who he says he is, does what he says he's doing, and will be with me for the long haul is different for me. Because of those scars from my failed marriage, Tom has to keep reminding me that this relationship is a good kind of different."

"I had to realize that the hurts of Megan's past affect us as a couple," Tom says. "I need to regularly reassure her and make sure she feels secure and safe. I also have scars from my first marriage—accusations of being the cause of every problem. So Megan reassures me that I'm not a failure or the problem, especially when differences arise between us."

Tom and Megan acknowledge their similarities and differences, but they also work hard to discover how those differences can actually strengthen their relationship. They have realized that one of them shouldn't always be the only one to change—both of them work things out as a team.

Remember when I (Susan) said earlier that Dale and I are both non-confrontational by nature? Because of this, there were times in our previous marriages when we both felt disrespected, used, and abused, and though we knew giving in all the time was unhealthy and poor modeling for our kids, we didn't know how to change or correct our behavior. Looking back now, we can see that in our previous marriages, we and our respective spouses never were a team, so we felt anger and resentment toward them. When our marriages dissolved, both of us knew that if we were ever to marry again, teamwork and a willingness to compromise or change had to be a strong mutual desire.

In the process of adjusting to differences, each individual must be intentional to avoid devaluing his or her partner's uniqueness. A critical spirit is a relationship killer. Judging, comparing, and rejecting the other person's behavior just because it's different from yours will only cause defensiveness, insecurity, frustration, and hurt, so avoid these at all costs. Sometimes it's best to simply choose to accept a difference rather than criticize it.

Focus on your loved one's strengths and what caused you to fall in love—the good things, the fun things, the positive things. When differences really bug you, remember that you're a team, and work together to solve the problems you may face.

Gender Differences

Men and women have unique strengths and gifts. In many cases, women tend to be better nurturers and emotionally care more deeply, while men often excel at being protectors and providers. The differences between men and women complement each other and can help establish balance when factored into a relationship setting.

"Our biggest challenges are those gender differences that so many couples face," Megan says. "When we have a conflict, I like to talk things through and work at it until it's all settled."

"I can talk it through for just so long," Tom says, "then I hit a limit and need a break. She'd rather stick with it and resolve it no matter how long it takes."

Women tend to be more emotional and detail oriented and are great at multitasking. They are usually more social and interdependent, and they need love and affirmation to feel secure and cared for. They often express their feelings freely, respond emotionally, and become personally invested in situations more easily than men.

"I'm way more worried about relational things," Megan says, "but Tom is more concerned about the kids' cars running well and stuff like that. It's just a girl-guy thing, I think. For us, it's also how our love languages work."

Men are often more logical, see things in generalities, and can compartmentalize more easily, so they can tackle tasks and solve problems well—like Tom keeping the cars running. They need to be respected for these traits as well as to feel loved.

"Unfortunately, because we have so many similarities, we also have the same weaknesses," Megan says. "We both tend to be late, forget birthdays, or mix up the schedule."

"We don't balance ourselves as much as people with different strengths and weaknesses do," Tom says. "But we do forgive each other quickly."

The way God wired you as a man and a woman can be a blessing in disguise. Sure, there may be times when you find those differences a mystery—even a bit weird—but there are also things you can appreciate about them. Dale appreciates that I (Susan) love to entertain and plan our trips, while I appreciate his support, acceptance, and even enjoyment of the social things we do.

When we observe the differences between men and women, we see the amazing and creative ways God made us different. And He can use those differences to teach us to be more like Him.

Personality Differences

In everyday life, the simple differences in personalities can get pretty irritating at times. There are introverts who marry extroverts, neatniks who marry slobs, savers who marry spenders. But those differences can also teach us many valuable lessons.

"I like things neat and tidy; I'll tackle a job and do what I can to get it done," Megan says. "Though we're both perfectionists, Tom is more so. It paralyzes him when he can't get things done right, so he tends to let things go until he can do them perfectly."

Personalities differ in many ways, so it's important to adjust to your partner's different preferences and needs. One example of this is dealing with different socializing preferences.

"Tom can get emotionally saturated and overwhelmed in a big group pretty quickly," Megan says.

"I'd rather have just a few people over and spend quality time with them," Tom admits. "But Megan's family likes big gatherings—the more the merrier! Though I'm not really an introvert, I just prefer socializing in smaller groups. When big groups gather, I tend to back away and do something on my own."

"But both of us have actually grown to appreciate the other's preference," Megan says. "I'm enjoying more one-on-one time, and I've found that I've missed out on building those intimate relationships. And Tom has learned to adjust and enjoy large gatherings—occasionally. It's been a learning experience for both of us."

"What I like most is that I've gained a whole new family," Tom says. "Megan's family has become my family, and it's great. I love her extended family, and they accept me as their own."

People sure are different! One of you might be optimistic and the other pessimistic. One might be a strict disciplinarian and the other a permissive parent. You could be reserved and your future mate spontaneous. Perhaps you're a talker and he's a quiet guy. Or maybe you're a morning dove and she's a night owl. Whatever your differences may be, you can work them out by lovingly negotiating your interests, needs, and desires.

To do this, avoid being overly critical and understand that the differences in your personalities and interests are part of both you and your future mate. Discuss your differences and be flexible and accommodating. But be sure to balance each other so neither of you does all the flexing—and make sure your relationship always takes precedence over your differences.

Different Backgrounds

Family and background differences can create issues, but they can also be assets. Our childhood, family, education, and all our past experiences collide to form who we are today and who we will become. Our attitudes and choices also form some of our differences.

"I grew up in a doctor's family, and we were Catholic," Tom says. "I'm the only one divorced in my family, so it took me more than six months to finally tell them. I felt like a failure."

"I was raised in a middle-class home and lived a simpler life," Megan says. "For Tom and me, our families of origin were very similar in some ways, but our first marriages and family lives were quite different."

Adjusting to your background differences can be a learning experience. Yet if you respect each other's past, serve one another lovingly despite your differences, and value the lessons each of you has learned through life's experiences, you'll be an emotionally healthy couple and will allow space for each other to grow.

"Tom always did a lot of activities with his kids," Megan says, "but I always had a lot of talk time with my kids. We played games, watched movies, and went on walks together. Blending these two different lifestyles has been challenging."

"Megan's kids spend time with us talking and hanging out," Tom says, "but my kids want to 'do stuff' together. We are always busy—one way or the other."

"Tom loves sports—hunting, golfing, fishing," Megan says, "but I love to watch movies, especially chick flicks."

"Megan loves to have the television on all the time," Tom says, "but that distracts me. I like quiet."

"So we both have had to compromise on these differences—a lot," Megan says. "I think we both give and take pretty fairly. But at first we didn't; we dealt with our differences very ungracefully."

"When we first got married, we 'compromised' by getting annoyed and having a lot of arguments," Tom says.

"For a while, we just didn't have the television on when we were together," Megan says. "But when Tom was traveling, I'd have the television on all the time. Then, when he was home and he left the table to go and do something, I decided to fill that void with the television. I responded out of annoyance, and that wasn't good. We needed to find balance and remember to think of the other more than ourselves. So now I limit my TV viewing, and Tom tries to stay more focused when we're together."

It comes down to loving each other enough to respect your partner's history and the experiences that make your future mate who he or she is. Though some things may be perplexing or take a lot of discussion, each of you can work toward keeping them from hindering your relationship.

Financial Differences

For second-marriage couples, finances often carry a lot of baggage, as well as reveal lifestyle differences and challenges that may require some adjustments. We'll talk more about this topic in chapter 8, but for now, we'll let Tom and Megan share a few of their financial differences.

"When we married, we combined our finances," Tom says. "But we had to decide how to make things work together. We differed on the way we viewed saving for retirement and handling some of our bills, so we had to work through those differences."

"Our finances were pretty even when we married, but I was naturally more of a saver," Megan says. "I had some money from the divorce, so we balanced our finances fairly well. But Tom would spend his money more freely, while I'd put it away for retirement. We just viewed finances a little differently."

"She's such a saver that I have to encourage her to go get what we need," Tom says, "except when it comes to the grandkids."

"When I lost my job, we had a big decision to make," Megan says. "We were remodeling the house, so it was important for one of us to be

Let Your Differences Work for You

More than any other Bible passage, Ephesians 4:2–3 can help you make your differences as a second-marriage couple work for you instead of against you. It says, "Be completely humble and gentle; be patient, bearing with one another in love. Make every effort to keep the unity of the Spirit through the bond of peace."

Here's how to apply this scriptural advice to your relationship:

    Be humble. Realize that your way of doing things may not always be the best way. Your future mate's way may not be either. Sometimes it's best to work together to find a new way to do something.

    Be gentle. When a difference makes you crazy, be gentle as you discuss it. Remember that differences are a part of the one you love, and your relationship is much more important than the way you do something.

    Be patient. You are on a lifelong journey of learning and growing together. It takes time to unlearn old habits and learn new ones. Sometimes you just need to learn to live with a difference—you bear with it, as Ephesians says. But that doesn't mean you grudgingly put up with that difference and make your future spouse feel bad about it. Instead, you love him or her in spite of it.

    Keep the unity and peace. Differences can make you feel disunited and steal the peace from your relationship, if you let them. Trust God's Spirit to help you find peace when differences threaten to tear your relationship apart.

Be sensitive and recognize that some of your differences are actually gifts. It's all in the way you choose to view those differences.

there when workers were there. So we decided that I would stay home. But adjusting to one income was hard for me."

"Megan is so handy," Tom says. "It made more sense for her to be there and do the house stuff."

"That let Tom be free to go and do his work without distraction," Megan says. "We could actually make more money with me staying home, and that empowered him to go and do a good job at work."

"I had never received a bonus until Megan stayed home," Tom says. "The bonuses I now get are more than Megan could ever make working outside the home, so it all works out well."

"My job is to keep 'life' running so Tom can go to work and not worry about anything," Megan says. "I run the errands, keep up with family, do appointments, that kind of thing. It works. But I must admit that it's also weird. Sometimes I feel like a freeloader and a little displaced, but I know Tom doesn't feel that way about me. I never want him to feel that I'm taking advantage of him, so we just have to keep talking about it and reassuring each other of our roles."

The complexities of second-marriage finances also raise questions of prenuptial agreements, wills, and trusts. Though each couple is different, these details are important to discuss, and we'll cover them more extensively in chapter 8.

As a second-marriage couple, Tom and Megan have learned how to work with their differences and use them to strengthen their marriage. You can too.

☘ BLENDING WITH KIDS

How Do You Deal with Different Parenting Styles?
When Tom and Megan got married, their kids ranged from their teens to their midtwenties. Megan had three kids, and Tom had three. And now they are grandparents to three . . . and counting.

"We've had it relatively easy when it comes to our kids, I think," Tom says. "Two of my children love and honor Megan. But one of my children has stronger loyalties to her mom."

"I think she felt that her closeness to her dad was being invaded when I entered the picture," Megan says. "To be honest, I was a little jealous because she and Tom were so close. But I needed to get over it and respect their relationship. As time passed, the tension lessened. My relationship with Tom's youngest daughter, Christy, was very different from my relationship with his other daughter. Christy lived with us for our first year of marriage. People suggested we wait and marry after Christy graduated from high school, but we chose to go ahead and marry then. Because we did, Christy and I have a very special bond, so it was a good thing!"

It's a good thing Megan recognized her feelings of jealousy and chose to respect the relationship between her husband and his daughter. Since jealousy can cause resentment toward someone because of a perceived advantage that he or she has, it often puts a wedge between people and can hurt everyone involved. To resolve any jealous feelings that may crop up, here are a few suggestions:

1. Check your own insecurity level, don't compare yourself or your situation to others, and remember that you are a child of God and your actions should reflect that.

2. Refuse to feel threatened, suspicious, fearful, envious, or resentful—none of these emotions are healthy or beneficial to you or your family members.

3. Trust your spouse and be realistic about the difficulties and adjustments that come with blending a family.

4. Give the situation to God through prayer and ask God to give you an extra measure of unselfishness.

5. Refocus. Philippians 4:8 says, "Finally, brothers, whatever is true, whatever is noble, whatever is right, whatever is pure, whatever is lovely, whatever is admirable—if anything is excellent or praiseworthy—think about such things."

"Megan's taught me a lot," Tom tells us. "I've learned to put my foot down when I need to, to back off when it's important, and to let the kids fail when they need to learn a lesson. Megan has also helped me set healthy boundaries."

"We've had to figure out how to manage Tom's authoritarian parenting style with the more relaxed parenting style I have," Megan says.

"We parented very differently," Tom says. "I was a rescuer, so if anyone needed anything, I'd drop everything to 'save' them."

"I'm the tough guy when it comes to the kids," Megan says. "I always tried to guide them so they'd be able to do it on their own—I'd let them fail and learn by it."

"Megan is the best mom I've ever seen," Tom says. "Right from the start, she was so wise to make sure her children knew that she really loved me, and she expected them to respect me. Unfortunately, I didn't do that, and that made things harder."

"Tom's children could be disrespectful to him at times, and they expected more because they had always gotten more. So they often put him in a position of choosing between them or me," Megan says. "It was an adjustment for all of us."

"Even though they were older and already out of the house when we married, Megan's kids truly love me as a dad, and I feel the same way about them," Tom says. "My children have a stronger loyalty toward their mother, as they should, but this has gotten in the way of them accepting my relationship with Megan."

"And of course, our former spouses factor into our relationships with the kids," Megan says. "One of our exes is more laid back and fine with the children spending time with Tom and me. But the other ex doesn't feel that way and often makes the kids feel guilty for spending time or enjoying their time with us, so that causes tension all the way around."

For Megan and Tom, their different parenting styles and the differences in their adult children's views of their relationship as a couple have had a long-lasting effect on their ability to blend their family. Though they love all of their kids, it isn't easy to work through the exes' influences, the individual mind-sets of their adult children, and the complexities of blending a family. As Tom says, "We're still a work in progress."

"One of the most wonderful things about second marriages is grandkids. There's no 'step' in grandparenting," Megan says. "This is a difference between the generations, I think. It's another piece of God's redemption, and I love it! There's no such thing as a step-grandparent in a child's eyes, and it's a beautiful new aspect of family life."

Here are some tips for working on your blending-family differences:

1. Learn to view your blending family, each day, with fresh, eager eyes, and don't expect perfection.

2. Don't ignore differences. Identify them and learn what makes each of you tick by studying your differences. And be open; you might discover that you like your future spouse's way of doing something better.

3. Evaluate and negotiate. Choose to grow in areas where you are different, and appreciate each individual. If a difference is a bad habit, an unhealthy behavior, or a destructive pattern that will negatively affect your family, set healthy boundaries.

4. Discover how God can use your differences. You don't have to view your differences as incompatible or irreconcilable. Reconcile your differences with love.

5. Embrace change. Changing old habits and learning new things is good. Read books together about your differences. Set goals that will bring family unity.

Differences can be challenging, but they can also help you grow as individuals and as a couple like few things can. Embrace the challenge to find peace and contentment within your differences. After all, you're one of a kind: God made you that way!

☘ APPRAISING MY LIFE

Think about areas in your life that differ from your future spouse's experience or personality. How will the two of you adjust to these differences? Are you both willing to sacrifice your own ideas, habits, and so on, to serve each other and become compatible, or will you fight change? Will your future mate fight change? Understand that marriage will mean a lot of change. It'll mean giving up your rights to many things, and that's okay. It'll also mean you may have to struggle through some tough issues and learn to compromise.

☘ ASSESSING OUR LIVES

Check out the following list, and then name five major differences you and your future spouse might struggle with in your marriage. Choose to work as a team to find solutions for these differences before you marry. Talk about how you can find common ground. Pray together, asking God for help embracing and reconciling these differences.

Do you and your future mate have differences in any of these areas?

- goals
- communication styles
- decision making
- social needs
- financial philosophies
- role expectations
- your family structure
- views about family
- parenting styles
- lifestyles
- family traditions
- weaknesses or faults

- physical needs
- emotional needs
- spiritual views
- relationships with in-laws

🌱 A MOMENT FOR FUN!

Which is your favorite season of the year and why?

What do you think your spiritual gift is (leadership, serving, teaching, giving, mercy, etc.)?

🌱 APPLYING GOD'S WORD

What does God say about the differences you and your future mate have?

> Do to others as you would have them do to you. (Luke 6:31)

> May the God who gives endurance and encouragement give you a
> spirit of unity among yourselves as you follow Christ Jesus, so that
> with one heart and mouth you may glorify the God and Father of our
> Lord Jesus Christ. Accept one another, then, just as Christ accepted
> you, in order to bring praise to God. (Romans 15:5–7)

There are different kinds of gifts, but the same Spirit. There are different kinds of service, but the same Lord. There are different kinds of working, but the same God works all of them in all men. (1 Corinthians 12:4–6)

You, my brothers, were called to be free. But do not use your freedom to indulge the sinful nature; rather, serve one another in love. (Galatians 5:13)

Be completely humble and gentle; be patient, bearing with one another in love. Make every effort to keep the unity of the Spirit through the bond of peace. (Ephesians 4:2–3)

8

Finances Are Complicated

How Do You Manage Your Finances?

*M*oney can cause more problems in marriage than most of us realize. Because Marcos and Isabel knew this, they decided to take lots of time to talk through the many details of their financial lives early on in their relationship. Since Marcos had one daughter and Isabel had two, the girls' needs were also considered as they moved toward their wedding day.

"It was important for us to find out each other's financial history before we got married," Isabel says. "We wanted to lay the groundwork for a healthy financial life together. That made things so much easier, and we've avoided a lot of potential problems."

As Marcos and Isabel attest, the most important time to discuss your financial affairs is before you get married. Because second-marriage finances are often very complicated, it's also wise to seek good financial counsel when you need it.

To avoid the stresses that money can bring to your marriage, learn about the spending and saving habits of your future spouse as well as his or her overall attitude toward money. Also be sure to learn all you can about your future mate's financial history and present debts or obligations. Then make a plan of action as to how you're going to handle your finances together.

Yet even when you do all the right preparation and talk everything through, life can change. In our situation, Susan had a well-paying job for the first several years of our marriage. But the stress of the job as well as her desire to do more writing led us to make a huge financial decision.

After lots of prayer and discussion, Susan and I (Dale) counted the cost of Susan starting her own business, and we decided together to make the change. It meant that she'd lose her salary and reduce our income by more than half, and I would financially support both of us as she moved to writing full-time. Though it's been an adjustment and we've had to make a new budget and cut back expenses, making such a big decision together was a great experience for both Susan and me, and reaching a unified decision made all the difference in moving forward.

Money Attitudes

All of us have attitudes about money, and most of us acquired our views of money from our parents. But our culture, the media, and our close friends and extended family can also influence us. And a death or divorce can cause fear, debt, uncertainty, mistrust, or other financial challenges that may affect a second marriage if we don't deal with those issues up front.

"I learned financial discipline from my parents—to pay for things as I went," Marcos says. "I've lived on a budget as long as I can remember. Before Isabel and I married, I used an online budget program and allocated just so much for each item, and I stuck by my plan. I even used pie charts!"

"My budgeting was not as tight," Isabel says. "When we married, I had some debt, so we decided to do a 'yours, mine, and ours' financial plan. We opened a joint account and paid the joint bills with that. But we kept our other personal stuff—my debt and his child support and other expenses—separate. This way worked best for us."

"We wanted to be responsible for our own past financial obligations so that we would be fair to each other," Marcos says. "But we continually work together to tweak our joint budget."

"Since we've married, things like buying an RV and paying the insurance have become a joint affair," Isabel says. "As time passes, more and more things are becoming joint."

How did your parents, as well as you and your former spouse, handle money? Your financial experiences will affect your marriage, so it would be wise for you to discuss these questions together as soon as you can.

Both Susan and I (Dale) had parents who grew up during the Depression, and both of us had mothers who became widows while we were children. These experiences greatly affected the way we view money, but thankfully, we realized early on that our views about saving and being secure financially were very similar. Being on the same page when it comes to financial decisions has worked well for us.

How have your life experiences as individuals affected your views of money? Take a few minutes and answer the following questions about your family of origin:

- Did you grow up rich, poor, or middle class?
- Were you secure or insecure about money?
- Did your family have money secrets or difficulties, or was there never enough?
- Did you see generosity, good shopping habits, and careful planning in your family?
- Was work more important than family or having fun more important than wise money management?
- Did family members gamble, overspend, or have a keeping-up-with-the-Joneses mentality?
- Were there emergency savings, tithing, charitable giving, and paying off credit cards monthly?

- Did your family recycle, sacrifice when needed, save, invest, or use coupons?
- Did your family expect to have the latest fashions, the newest technology, club memberships, new vehicles, furniture, and travel—even when they couldn't afford it?
- Does peer pressure tend to push you to live beyond your means?

Now, go back and answer the questions according to your previous marriage experiences. What will you change in your second-marriage financial life?

All these attitudes and experiences directly or indirectly influence the way you think about money. Assess their positive or negative influences on your life to determine your views regarding money and finances.

Different Dynamics

Hebrews 13:5 says, "Keep your lives from the love of money and be content with what you have." There are many levels of spenders and savers, and although you and your future spouse can be different and still compatible, it's good to understand how different you are when it comes to money management. The extremes can create a very stressful marriage.

"Marcos is more of a saver, but we're both quite frugal," Isabel says. "Neither of us is extravagant. We manage our finances so we can pay cash for almost everything."

"Isabel likes to record every detail and balance things so she knows exactly how much we have," Marcos says, "but I like to see finances through percentages. We are both frugal and like financial planning, but we do it in different ways."

"I've always done my own finances," Isabel says, "and now we work on our finances as a couple. We constantly set and revise the financial goals we're working toward. One of our financial goals was for me to be able to retire from teaching, and that just happened."

If one of you spends a lot and needs the latest brand-name fashions, wants to eat out a lot, or loves to shop, while the other wants to save every penny, there is bound to be conflict. Though Marcos and Isabel don't have to deal with these extremes like many couples do, they still make it a point to discuss their financial purchases regularly.

"We are both planners," Isabel says. "We talk about all our purchases, whether small or big—and we trust each other."

"I saved up to buy a truck with cash," Marcos says. "So now we're reaping the benefits of not having truck payments."

"If I need something, I can buy it because we just aren't extravagant with our purchases," Isabel says.

"That's part of the flexibility of trusting each other and having a joint account plus his-and-hers accounts," Marcos says. "As long as we're open and honest with what we do, and we make respectful, joint decisions, we don't need to worry."

Understanding each other's money priorities and views can defuse many disagreements. But that's only half the battle. Self-discipline and restraint are also critical components of money management. Together you need to come to a mutual agreement on how much you will spend and save, what sacrifices you will make, and what priorities you will establish. And when kids—and all their financial obligations—are involved, it can get pretty complicated!

"Since I've retired from teaching, I'm free to travel and do a few more things than Marcos," Isabel says. "So we have to figure out how to manage that, because he's still working and has limited vacation time."

"There are always tweaks we need to make," Marcos says, "so we're always making those adjustments. We're thankful for what we have, and we find a good balance together. Part of that balance is to keep on planning, setting goals, and dreaming. We may not be rich financially, but we're rich in our life together."

God ordained that we should be good stewards and manage our

resources well. He wants us to acquire money honestly (Proverbs 13:11), invest it carefully (Matthew 25:16; Luke 14:28), spend it wisely (Proverbs 21:5), and share it joyfully (2 Corinthians 9:7; Acts 4:32–35). Couples who find ways to do this well will thrive financially.

Financial Danger Signs

Financial dangers will affect your second marriage unless you deal with them early. Finding solutions to these problems before you marry will help your relationship be more peaceful.

For second-marriage couples, the exes can often be the cause of financial difficulties, and so can the alimony and child-support payments. Many couples we've counseled have come into their second marriage with debt or huge financial obligations from their previous marriages. Whatever the case may be, challenges such as these can cause stress if you don't figure out how to manage them.

Others may find that their future mate has poor money-management skills or unhealthy money attitudes that need to be addressed. If one of you has insufficient income to pay the bills, refuses to balance the checkbook regularly, has a get-rich-quick attitude, or is unwilling to work hard to make ends meet, these are signs of unhealthy financial thinking. Other bad money habits are borrowing beyond your means or making purchases on credit while paying only the minimum payment on a revolving credit account. These are warning signs of poor stewardship, and it's best to work through these problems early. An irresponsible financial attitude will certainly haunt you and hurt your relationship.

The Demon of Debt

Let's discuss a four-letter word that can really hurt a relationship: DEBT. Debt is simply everything you owe. It could be your rent or mortgage, car payments or school loans, credit-card debt, or late utility bills. In our consumer culture, the list of perceived "must haves" just keeps growing, and many people are willing to purchase those things even if they must pay for them on credit. And any credit that's not paid off every month is debt.

As you can guess, Marcos and Isabel tend to avoid debt like the plague. But like most couples, they do have a mortgage, and in this economy, that too can cause stress.

"Before we married, a lot of our financial discussions were about where we would live," Isabel says. "We both had our own homes, so we decided to sell them and buy one house together. We needed to live in the school district where Marcos's daughter is enrolled, so we found a house in an area that would work for us.

"Marcos and I worry about the economy," Isabel tells us, "so we wrestle a lot with this mortgage-debt issue. Should we move and downsize? We're still not sure, because the economy dictates our plans. So for now, we just have to be content and let things happen in God's time."

Besides a mortgage, the average household today has more than fifteen thousand dollars in credit-card debt![1] And unfortunately, statistics show that 43 percent of United States households spend more than they earn annually.[2] Determine now not to be a couple who falls into this money trap. For more information on this important subject, Scott and Bethany Palmer's book *First Comes Love, Then Comes Money* can help.

Finding the Balance

Marcos and Isabel have learned that the pathway to financial freedom is one of discipline and proactive planning. There are steps you can take to change the way you think about—and use—money. If you're in debt, the first step to becoming successful financially is to take a hard look at your financial history and understand how you got into the situation. If mistakes have been made, ask God for forgiveness, strength, courage, and wisdom to help you change your attitudes and behavior. Discuss with your future spouse the changes that need to be made to move forward with a healthier perspective.

The Bible says that "the love of money is a root of all kinds of evil" (1 Timothy 6:10). Money itself isn't evil, but loving it often causes us to become greedy or financially reckless. There are many other biblical guidelines for managing money. One is to understand that everything belongs to God (Hebrews 13:5; Psalm 50:12). We have to realize we're just stewards of what really belongs to God.

"We took a premarital class and read several books together," Isabel says. "During the class, we talked a lot about our financial pasts and present, how we do things, who had debt, that sort of thing. We wanted to be sure our financial lives were both in order."

It takes work, but once you've changed your thinking, how do you become good stewards of what God has given you, and how do you blend both the finances and attitudes toward money that you bring into your second marriage?

Here's how to start:

1. List all your income, expenses, and debt individually. Turn to the end of this chapter now and complete your personal "Appraising My Life" financial assessment. Be honest and accurate because this will show you your true financial status.

2. Create a budget. Using the financial assessments you performed individually, you can now develop a budget for your marriage by turning to the end of this chapter and completing the "Assessing Our Lives" financial budget. This will help you establish spending limits as well as set financial priorities and goals. Be sure to include all your kids' expenses. Your budget should be the control engine of your money-management plan.

3. Establish realistic goals for getting out of debt. List actions that must be changed in order to correct, or strengthen, your

financial situation. Set a time limit to accomplish these goals. Remember, it took you awhile to get into debt, and it may take longer to get out of it. Pray for patience and use all the discipline you can muster.

4. To accomplish your financial goals, you need to set priorities. Eliminating credit cards may be your first priority. First, tackle paying off the cards with the highest interest. To stop the misuse of credit cards, distinguish carefully between your wants and your needs, and even your children's needs and wants. If you explore why you think you need or want something, you may be surprised how many wants can be eliminated.

5. Monitor your progress, especially your spending. You may be shocked to recognize some unhealthy spending habits you may have. Establish strict boundaries to begin new healthy money habits. Track daily expenses, down to cups of coffee or candy purchases—they all add up. Two daily trips to Starbucks can cost you hundreds of dollars a month! This will be very informative when you compare income to expenses.

6. Celebrate (in some reasonable way) when you achieve a financial goal.

Though finances aren't always easy to discuss, start early and be open and honest as you make your financial life together a successful one. And remember that your attitude about money is what's important, not the amount of money you have. Talk through money issues and strategically work together to find wise solutions to the challenges you may encounter. Philippians 4:6 will help you along the way: "Do not be anxious about anything, but in everything, by prayer and petition, with thanksgiving, present your requests to God."

As Susan and I (Dale) move toward retirement in a time of recession, we realize that this uncertain economy brings special challenges. We regularly review our finances and adjust as needed, but we know that, ultimately, we have to ask God for guidance, use our finances wisely, and not be anxious about the days to come.

Money should be a source of comfort, not stress, and it can be if you and your future spouse find solutions together. It will strengthen the bond between you and build trust, intimacy, and love.

Second-Marriage Complexities

Prenuptial agreements are popular in today's culture. But we want to encourage you to consider your motivations and all your options before you move forward with these types of decisions. It's understandable that before you remarry, you may want to protect your children's interests or make sure you reserve money to care for aging parents. In these cases, we would recommend you consider forming a legal trust or detailed will instead of going the route of a prenuptial agreement. Though a prenuptial agreement might protect your assets—if you divorce—the fact is that it can also be problematic for your relationship. From what we've experienced and seen when counseling couples, we think forming a trust (or trusts) is a much more secure way to go.

"When Isabel and I were dating," Marcos says, "we weren't able to be together a lot during the week, so we would read our premarital material over the phone and discuss it. We talked about a lot of things, especially finances. Through it all, we learned that we really could trust each other, so we decided not to make a prenuptial agreement. That's been a good decision for us.

"When Isabel and I married, we started to change my will, but we soon realized it was just too complicated," Marcos tells us. "When there are his-and-hers kids, as well as stuff from the past, often a will won't do. So through a lot of discussion, we decided to create a trust. That gave us more flexibility as well as good protection."

"I never had a will," Isabel says, "so all of this was quite a learning curve for me. It was a long and emotional process. We wanted to take care of our children and each other upon one of our deaths. It was a lot of work, but it was well worth it."

"In creating our trust, we decided to divide our inheritances evenly between our three girls," Marcos says. "That way, they are all sisters equally."

"Part of blending our family was blending our finances wisely," Isabel says. "We wanted to give the girls a legacy that they are all our daughters. Having a trust gave us a sense of security, and we told our girls about it. Going through this process has not only solidified our finances; it solidified our family."

"It's an ongoing process and will continue to be, I'm sure," Marcos says. "These past five years have brought a lot of change, so we have to keep on changing with time."

Yes, second-marriage finances tend to be complicated. But discussing these issues and planning ahead will help pave the way to a smoother financial life together. Each of your financial journeys will look different from other couples, and that's okay. What's important is that you create a financial plan that is right for both of you.

☘ BLENDING WITH KIDS

What about Kids and Money?

As you've read, all of the couples in this book have faced unique challenges with kids. And money is one of them. For some, one set of kids may be used to getting lots of name-brand gifts and receiving large amounts of money, while their stepsiblings may be used to Kraft-dinner frugality. Blending these extremes can be a struggle, and it can take a lot of discussion between the two of you. Sometimes you may even need outside counsel to help.

Since our children were young adults when Susan and I (Dale) married, we decided to keep our children's and grandchildren's expenses separate. Financially, I helped with my son's wedding; Susan helped her daughter with hers. Each of our five children has his or her own unique needs that we choose to respond to. My three sons are scattered across the country, while Susan's daughter is a missionary in South Africa and her son is still single. We've both helped our children and grandchildren along the way, and that's okay.

Although each couple will view how they want to interact with children and finances differently, just be sure you decide ahead of time and are in agreement with how you choose to do it, making sure it doesn't negatively affect your marriage and your joint finances.

Some couples also face the stresses of an ex's financial demands, whether from child support, unreasonable financial expectations, or unexpected situations that no one can predict. As a second-marriage couple, don't let these kinds of outside influences pull you apart. Work as a team to overcome them.

Other couples can blend their family's finances fairly easily. Much of it depends on what the children are used to, how old your children are, and what your current financial situation is.

When Marcos and Isabel married, Marcos's daughter was a teenager and lived with them half-time, so he anticipated all the expenses that a teenage girl brings to the family budget, including future college expenses. Isabel's two daughters were already in college, so she had those expenses and the weddings to come. So Marcos and Isabel decided to provide separately for their own children's financial needs at this stage in their lives.

"Marcos and I have had all three girls live with us at one time or another," Isabel says, "as well as our son-in-law and grandson! Marcos's daughter lived with us for several years. My oldest daughter lived with us for a year and a half. Then my younger daughter and her family moved in for a few months until they found a new house."

"But it's been a blessing," Marcos says, "because they all became family and got to experience us as a married couple. All three of the girls are *my* girls, and though the finances might be separate, there is no 'step' to our relationships. We are one blended family."

For some blending families, keeping finances separate may not be feasible. Some of the couples we've counseled have chosen to live on one income so that either Dad or Mom can stay home with the kids. Other couples kept child support, alimony, and the like separate and used certain funds only for their children. For one engaged couple, the woman had a lot of debt related to her child, so she and her fiancé decided to postpone their wedding until she had paid down her debt. Whatever your circumstances may be, be proactive and carefully decide together how your finances are going to work regarding your children.

🌿 APPRAISING MY LIFE

Complete your own personal financial portrait separately before developing a budget together for your marriage. Fill in the *His* and *Hers* blanks in the Current Financial Statement section in "Assessing Our Lives." As you work together to create a budget for your family, the following suggested budget percentages can help:

- Housing (including rent/mortgage and utilities): 25–30%
- Food: 10%
- Auto: 15%
- Tithe: 10%
- Savings: 5–10%
- Debt: 5%
- Insurance: 5%
- Medical: 5%
- Clothing: 5%
- Recreation/entertainment: 5%
- Miscellaneous: 5%
  Total: 100%

❦ ASSESSING OUR LIVES

Prepare a financial budget together for when you're married. (Note: If you tend to be an impulsive buyer, set a limit for discretionary buying. Limit your purchases to under fifty dollars (or only what you can afford after doing your budget). Anything over that, discuss it together, budget for it, delay your purchase, wait for a sale, or decide not to buy it.)

CURRENT FINANCIAL STATEMENT

Income per Month   Marriage Budget

Salary: his _____ hers _____ ours _____

Other income (interest,
dividends, alimony,
support, etc.):   his _____ hers _____ ours _____

Gross Income: his _____ hers _____ ours _____

Subtract from Gross Income

Tithe/charitable giving: his _____ hers _____ ours _____

Savings: his _____ hers _____ ours _____

Other: his _____ hers _____ ours _____

Spouse support/alimony: his _____ hers _____ ours _____

Total Income: his _____ hers _____ ours _____

Expenses per Month   Marriage Budget

Child expenses: his _____ hers _____ ours _____

   Child support   his _____ hers _____ ours _____

   Schooling   his _____ hers _____ ours _____

   Activities   his _____ hers _____ ours _____

   Other   his _____ hers _____ ours _____

Expenses per Month   **Marriage Budget**

Housing:

    Rent/mortgage/lease   his _____ hers _____ ours _____

    Insurance (renters or house) his _____ hers _____ ours _____

    Taxes   his _____ hers _____ ours _____

    Misc. (repairs, renovations) his _____ hers _____ ours _____

Utilities:

    Electricity   his _____ hers _____ ours _____

    Gas   his _____ hers _____ ours _____

    Water   his _____ hers _____ ours _____

    Sanitation   his _____ hers _____ ours _____

    Cable   his _____ hers _____ ours _____

    Trash   his _____ hers _____ ours _____

    Internet   his _____ hers _____ ours _____

    Phone (landline and cell) his _____ hers _____ ours _____

    Maintenance/repairs   his _____ hers _____ ours _____

    Other   his _____ hers _____ ours _____

Food:

    Groceries   his _____ hers _____ ours _____

    Eating out   his _____ hers _____ ours _____

Auto:

    Payments   his _____ hers _____ ours _____

    Taxes/license   his _____ hers _____ ours _____

    Gas   his _____ hers _____ ours _____

    Maintenance   his _____ hers _____ ours _____

    Replacement   his _____ hers _____ ours _____

    Insurance   his _____ hers _____ ours _____

Medical:

    Doctor   his _____ hers _____ ours _____

    Dentist   his _____ hers _____ ours _____

    Pharmacy   his _____ hers _____ ours _____

Expenses per Month   **Marriage Budget**

Insurance:

    Life   his _____ hers _____ ours _____

    Health   his _____ hers _____ ours _____

    Other   his _____ hers _____ ours _____

Debts:

    Credit cards

    (record each one)   his _____ hers _____ ours _____

    Loans

    Education   his _____ hers _____ ours _____

    Personal (friends/family) his _____ hers _____ ours _____

    Other   his _____ hers _____ ours _____

Entertainment:

    Movies

    (theater/video rental) his _____ hers _____ ours _____

    Trips   his _____ hers _____ ours _____

    Activities/sports   his _____ hers _____ ours _____

    Vacation   his _____ hers _____ ours _____

    Pets   his _____ hers _____ ours _____

    Other   his _____ hers _____ ours _____

Clothing:

    New purchases   his _____ hers _____ ours _____

    Alterations/dry cleaning his _____ hers _____ ours _____

Miscellaneous:

    Beauty/barber   his _____ hers _____ ours _____

    Toiletries/cosmetics his _____ hers _____ ours _____

    Lunch/allowances   his _____ hers _____ ours _____

    Furniture/household his _____ hers _____ ours _____

    Subscriptions/

    Memberships   his _____ hers _____ ours _____

    Gifts (including Christmas) his _____ hers _____ ours _____

Expenses per Month   **Marriage Budget**

School   his _____ hers _____ ours _____

Petty cash   his _____ hers _____ ours _____

Emergencies   his _____ hers _____ ours _____

Other   his _____ hers _____ ours _____

Total Expenses: his _____ hers _____ ours _____

Income vs. Expenses

Total income: his _____ hers _____ ours _____

Less total expenses: his _____ hers _____ ours _____

Discretionary funds (hopefully): his _____ hers _____ ours _____

☙ A MOMENT FOR FUN!

If you had a million dollars, what charity would you give it to and why?

What was the best job you ever had?

🌱 APPLYING GOD'S WORD

There are more than two thousand scriptures that speak about money and possessions, and that means this is a big issue for us—and for God. Here are just a few:

Wealth and honor come from you [God]. (1 Chronicles 29:12)

The wicked borrow and do not repay, but the righteous give generously. (Psalm 37:21)

Dishonest money dwindles away, but he who gathers money little by little makes it grow. (Proverbs 13:11)

All hard work brings a profit, but mere talk leads only to poverty. (Proverbs 14:23)

Better a little with the fear of the Lord than great wealth with turmoil. (Proverbs 15:16)

The plans of the diligent lead to profit as surely as haste leads to poverty. (Proverbs 21:5)

The rich rule over the poor, and the borrower is servant to the lender. (Proverbs 22:7)

Each man should give what he has decided in his heart to give, not reluctantly or under compulsion, for God loves a cheerful giver. (2 Corinthians 9:7)

My God will meet all your needs according to his glorious riches in Christ Jesus. (Philippians 4:19)

Godliness with contentment is great gain. For we brought nothing
into the world, and we can take nothing out of it. But if we have food
and clothing, we will be content with that. People who want to get
rich fall into temptation and a trap and into many foolish and harmful
desires that plunge men into ruin and destruction. For the love of
money is a root of all kinds of evil. (1 Timothy 6:6–10)

Keep your lives free from the love of money and be content with what
you have. (Hebrews 13:5)

9

Redemptive Intimacy

*What's God Design for Sexual Intimacy
in a Second Marriage?*

Karen grew up in an abusive, alcoholic home. Life wasn't easy for her. By the age of sixteen, she wanted to escape from the abuse so badly that she ran off and married a boy her own age. Karen immediately got pregnant, and the all-too-young marriage soon ended. Karen spent the next thirteen years as a single mom, raising her son and struggling to make it alone. After a second very difficult failed marriage, the betrayal she experienced from her ex's pornography addiction and adultery left Karen with a lot of emotional heartache. There were issues she needed to work through and find healing for in order to move forward in a healthy way.

"The betrayal of pornography on top of the affair was just too much to deal with," Karen says. "My ex-husband called himself a Christian, so I had a lot of confusion to overcome regarding faith and Christianity, and I had a lot of healing to do."

Paul didn't have it easy either. His ex was a meth user, so he had to protect his five-year-old daughter from her mother's addiction. But doing that on his own was more difficult than he could ever have imagined. Between all the legal issues and emotional challenges, Paul finally turned to God for help, and shortly after that, he became a Christian. Then he and Karen met and fell in love.

"I firmly believe that God was right in the middle of our relationship," Paul says. "Karen's the best thing ever—for me and for my daughter, Sarah."

The truth is, previous relationships leave indelible marks on each one of us. Some are good, but as with Karen and Paul, many are negative. And when our relationships leave marks on sexual intimacy that are powerful, deep, and personal, they can also bring good and bad memories and strong emotions.

Most second-marriage couples have experienced the reality of this. Unless some physical or emotional limitation prevented sexual intimacy in a previous marriage, more than likely sex has been a part of each person's life before they enter a second marriage. So that makes sexual intimacy both a challenge and a place where God can bring healing, hope, and redemption like few other areas of life can. God made us to be in relationship, and because marriage is the most intimate and intense of all relationships, it can be redemptive beyond words when it is done right. When we love, serve, and enjoy each other as God planned, and when covenant commitment undergirds all that, sexual intimacy can be an amazing and wonderful part of our lives.

"God provided us with a fresh start," Karen says, "and He can do that for you too. If you give your past to God and choose to have a new beginning, the area of sexual intimacy can be one of the most beautiful and redemptive areas of your marriage and your life."

"We've been married for almost five years," Paul says, "and we've experienced God's grace in this area of our marriage. We feel like it's a reward for making Him the foundation of our marriage."

"The redeeming power of remarriage is so evident to us," Karen says. "God makes all things new. We don't concentrate on looking back on the former things; instead, we experience God's love and grace in our marriage now."

For anyone going into a second marriage, it's wise to view sexual intimacy in your relationship as a place where God can give you a new start. Whether you've lost your first marriage to death or divorce, the fear of being intimate again can be overwhelming. Guilt, mistrust, isolation, or even shame can threaten to hinder intimacy. So first make sure you resolve whatever issues you might have with sexual intimacy, whether through prayer, discussion, or counseling, and then make a covenant with your future mate to give this area of your marriage to God. In the power of redemption, even the broken places of your life can be made new.

God's redemptive power was evident in our relationship early on. As I mentioned earlier, soon after Susan and I (Dale) got engaged, I was diagnosed with prostate cancer. My treatment options seemed worse than the cancer itself. The words "in sickness and in health" were tested even before we married. I had to offer Susan the chance to back out of the engagement. I soon found out how strong her love for me was as she stood by me through it all. Her unconditional love for me continues to be a blessing, and it laid the foundation for deep and wonderful intimacy—in all its forms.

Redemption and Reality

Sex within marriage should be a reflection of unselfish giving—not unlike the loving relationship Christ has with His church. It's about care, sacrifice, submission, devotion, tenderness, and respect. Making love is also about fun, pleasure, and enjoyment—and the reality of experiencing true intimacy. Sexual intimacy within marriage is also fulfilling, holy, honorable, healthy, and healing.

"You can make a choice to let your former emotional scars and relationships pull you down and put you in a prison of fear and hate and bitterness," Karen says, "or you can choose to break those chains and forgive and move on. Paul and I chose to live a rich life free from the past and walk in a way that pleases God."

"Past baggage may try to haunt us, but we just won't let it," Paul says. "Although it's really hard to forgive my ex for all she put my daughter and me through, I have to choose forgiveness, day by day."

"My ghosts of fear and poor self-esteem have caused me to want to run," Karen says. "And I had to admit that to Paul. I just wanted a peaceful, happy, and safe relationship, and I didn't want to bring my baggage into our new marriage."

"Karen's fears were intimidating to me," Paul admits, "but it was worth working with her to overcome those fears. I have never had anybody care for me like she does. In past relationships, it was always about the other person and what she wanted."

Baggage from a failed marriage—or from losing a spouse to death—can often cause people to have fears and concerns about this intimate part of their lives. If you still suffer the effects of sexual hurts, wounds, rejection, and the like, we suggest seeking professional help to assist you in overcoming them before you remarry.

Talking about Sex

Although you already know a lot about your future mate, the reality is, you'll spend your entire life getting to know him or her better. But in areas as deep and important as sexual intimacy, understanding how your future mate is created is very important.

So how can you tell—before marriage—if your partner has the same interest, attitude, and desire for sex as you do, without getting entangled in a sexual relationship prior to marriage? Naturally God made man and woman sexually compatible, and, barring any physical or psychological problems, sex is almost instinctive. If your future spouse is kind, giving, unselfish, and seeking your best, sex will be, most likely, a joyful journey of discovery. But if you choose to experiment before you marry, you'll be forfeiting a very special gift. In fact, saving sex for marriage is the best wedding present you can give each other.

"Early on, we shared all our hurts and painful pasts with each other," Karen says. "I had had breast cancer before I met Paul, so I had lots of scars and was afraid to tell him about them. Because my ex had pulled away from me because of those scars, I needed to share these fears with Paul."

"I told Karen that she should wear those scars with pride," Paul says. "They just don't matter to me."

"That was such a turning point for me," Karen notes. "God says that He will restore the things that have been lost, and He does! God used Paul's love and acceptance to heal so many of my past issues."

"I tell my friends that I'm a happily married man, and that's a badge of honor for me," Paul says. "Karen and I are grateful for our relationship, so we do our best to encourage and lift each other up."

"The more positives we have in our relationship," Karen says, "the more those negative things of the past just fade away. They become distant shadows. But making that happen is intentional—we choose to never, ever tear each other down. If Paul does something wrong, I tell him 'It's okay,' and he does the same. We all make mistakes, so we need to be gentle with one another. The premarital class we took gave us the tools to do this well."

"Continuing to learn all we can about having a healthy relationship helps us do things right," Paul says, "so we don't have to relive the past."

Intentionality is so important in this area of your lives. Intentionally avoiding premarital sex, intentionally dealing with your past and then leaving it behind, and intentionally building each other up and caring for one another. Do these things, and you'll build a strong and intimate relationship. Susan and I (Dale) determined to do all this, and we've never regretted it. You may even want to prepare for this more by reading material specific to sexual intimacy in marriage (see the reading list at the end of this book).

The Past, Present, and Future

Because so many factors affect the way you view sex, understanding your thoughts about it is important. You may have strong feelings about petting, foreplay, oral sex, negligees, bathing together, the need for cleanliness, and so on. Think about these things and assess why you feel the way you do about each topic.

Consider where your attitudes about sex came from. Your parents? School? Friends? Older siblings? Pornography, TV, movies, music, and other media? Previous relationships?

"My ex was addicted to pornography, and to me that was adultery," Karen says. "When I shared this with Paul, God really showed him what that concern was all about."

"I thought pornography was harmless," Paul says, "but my attitude about it changed pretty quickly. Where I work, there are a lot of inappropriate magazines around, but I intentionally keep them out of my view. And when I begin to think about how that photographed woman's father might feel—or how I would feel if it were my daughter—I feel convicted and crushed."

"Paul makes a point to look away when there's something on TV or in a movie that's not appropriate," Karen says. "I respect him so much for keeping his eyes pure. That's God honoring, and it honors me. It makes him more attractive to me."

"I choose to be single-focused. Karen cares about this, and she knows that I will keep my focus on her," Paul says. "If I'm driving down the street and there's an attractive woman riding a bike, I make a conscious choice to watch the road ahead. I choose to guard what I see. Doing this affects the way I see my wife, and it grows my desire for only her."

Take Paul's wisdom to heart. He's made some major lifestyle choices to change from worldly views of sex to a godly view of sexuality. In so doing, he's built trust, confidence, loyalty, and a special, intimate bond with his wife that wouldn't have been possible otherwise.

It all starts with a personal assessment. Were either of you promiscuous or involved in recreational sex or pornography in your past? Admission of moral failure is important, but specific details of your past sexual history don't necessarily need to be discussed with your fiancé(e). You should, however, make sure you're sensitive, honest, and open with your future mate so that any consequences of past actions (STDs, HIV-AIDS, addictions, etc.) can be resolved medically and/or emotionally.

Some of you may even have fears that this area of your second marriage won't be as good as your first, especially if you had a good marriage and lost your first spouse to death. Others who have never been married and are marrying someone who's experienced death or divorce may have worries as well. A session or two with a counselor should be able to help you work through such fears.

Issues such as sexual abuse, incest, molestation, promiscuity, or a pornography addiction may require more extensive therapy with your pastor or a professional Christian counselor. Other troubling sexual experiences may be resolved by talking with your pastor or a counselor, with or without your future spouse, so that full healing can be achieved. But know that with God's forgiveness and love, there is hope for those who've failed or been hurt in this area.

"God can heal you if you're open and honest and if you're willing to work at getting rid of the pain of the past and learning how to serve one another in a healthy way," Karen says. "Doing this is necessary so that you don't repeat the past."

Why Wait?

Sex before marriage can hinder and even damage your chance for real intimacy. Premarital sex only masquerades as love and intimacy, so don't be deceived by the myth that it's okay. The argument that you have to experience sex to understand it or be good at it is also a myth. Be careful not to fall prey to these traps, and if you have, know that you can start fresh today and choose to abstain until you marry.

"Sex is powerful," Karen says. "So if a problem arises and you need to break off or postpone the engagement, it's so much easier to walk away from the relationship if sex isn't a factor. You can see more clearly if there's something wrong. Sex before marriage simply clouds your judgment. So we knew that waiting was the right thing to do before God."

If you've been sexually active with each other, we urge you to stop and sincerely ask God and your partner for forgiveness. Then make a vow with each other to remain abstinent until you marry. First Corinthians 6:18–19 says, "Flee from sexual immorality. . . . Do you not know that your body is a temple of the Holy Spirit?" The fact that you've been sexually intimate doesn't mean your relationship is ruined. You can move forward toward having a great marriage if you will choose to make wise choices, set a good example for your children, and remain abstinent until your wedding day.

You may be afraid that if you choose to stop having premarital sex, your future mate will feel hurt or, worse, decide to end the relationship. This could happen, of course, but if it did, it would tell you that your future mate is marrying you for the wrong reasons. It's more likely that he or she will only have greater respect for you, for your future mate will see that you value him or her more than sexual gratification.

"I think many people, even Christians, have become desensitized to what sex does," Karen says. "I don't think couples realize how much it will crack the foundation of their relationship if they engage in sex before marriage."

As we discussed earlier, if you're living together, we strongly suggest changing your lifestyle by deciding that one of you will move out. Take time to know each other without sexual involvement and the daily intimacy of living in the same place, and make sure that you're both untangled from the past. We know this isn't easy or convenient, but it's worth it. The good news is that God's forgiveness in this area is available to you, and His grace can help you start your marriage in the right way.

"It's easy to just say, 'Oh, I've been married before, so it doesn't matter,'" Karen says, "but it does matter."

Waiting to have sex also builds trust, confidence, and loyalty in your relationship, and enhances bonding with your future mate. Matthew 5:8 says, "Blessed are the pure in heart, for they will see God." That includes purity not only sexually but also in the way you dress, in your behavior, and in your thought life. It's also important to remember that as a believer in Christ, obedience to God's Word should be a priority in your life. You want to begin your marriage with a strong moral foundation, and you want to display a healthy, godly relationship to your children.

Though it's hard, flee from tempting situations and too much sensual stimulation. You're attracted to each other, and you should be, but don't stoke the fires until your wedding night. Respect the one you love enough to keep him or her chaste until you marry.

Preparing for Intimacy

Sexual intimacy built on unselfishness and sacrifice makes your relationship strong, and it's pleasing to God. Controlling your sexual desires until they can be freely experienced within marriage is God's design. It also has a way of building security in your relationship, because you can see the inner strength of your partner in avoiding temptation.

"We both feel that we have a strong, satisfying sex life," Karen says. "But I think that's because we wanted to do things right from the beginning. We realized that if we honored God when it came to sex and our relationship, He would bless this part of our marriage, and He did!"

"Learn as much as you can about each other, but you don't have to share all the details of your past," Paul says. "And when you're married, make your partner the total focus of your sexual desire."

God designed our bodies to complement each other, to become aroused, to enjoy pleasure, and to hunger for one another sexually—romancing, kissing, touching, caressing, affirming, and more. Within marriage, sex can be both erotic and pure, passionate and holy, fun and honorable. And best of all, the two of you become one.

"Write down your hopes, desires, and dreams for what you expect intimately from each other so that you can understand and prepare," Karen says. "Don't hold anything back. Make the time to discuss these things—outside the bedroom—and avoid falling into having sex before marriage. If you understand the beauty of intimacy and the freedom God gives within marriage, it's a wonderful thing."

It's an intricate dance, to be sure. The key is to understand how your future mate is wired and then, when you marry, learn how to meet his or her needs. Sex is an all-encompassing act: It involves your physical, mental, emotional, and spiritual selves. And God is pleased in knowing His creation is enjoying what He created you to experience within marriage. He wants you to have fun, be free to indulge unashamed, and lavish in who and how He made both of you. The purpose of sex is to connect you as husband and wife on the deepest level possible, to make you completely safe and vulnerable together, and to enable you to experience a unique, exclusive closeness that no one else experiences with your mate.

Making love is a lifelong learning experience—it's about building intimacy physically, emotionally, psychologically, and spiritually. Your desires will ebb and flow—sometimes they will be stronger; other times they will be weaker—and they will be different for each of you. The various seasons of life, such as childbearing, childrearing, and menopause, will affect your sexual intimacy as well.

Sexual intimacy is a deep nonverbal expression of love that can only be fully realized in an atmosphere of safety and commitment. Within the context of marriage, sexual intimacy involves the mind, will, emotions, and body working together. It's also fun, holy, exciting, and life changing. Enjoy!

✿ BLENDING WITH KIDS

What about Sexual Intimacy with Children Around?
Enjoying sexual intimacy as second-marriage newlyweds when children are in the home can be quite a challenge. To plan for this, it's good to figure out how to handle your intimate moments before you remarry. Then make a plan of action.

"We gave Sarah her own special space downstairs, since our room would be upstairs," Paul says. "She was seven when we married, so I don't think she understood why we really did that."

"We felt more comfortable and less inhibited when little ears weren't listening," Karen says. "Couples who have children just down the hall have to set boundaries—and sometimes they might need to be a little creative."

"We want to model appropriate behavior for Sarah and set a good example," Paul says. "We are careful to be private with our sexual intimacy, but we also want to show her what a healthy relationship looks like."

"She's not allowed to come into our room without being invited," Karen says. "Our bedroom is our sanctuary. We can enjoy our privacy and know she'll respect those boundaries. We set that standard from the very beginning, and even at age seven, she obeyed the rules. Thankfully, the floors are so creaky that we can hear her coming!"

"Sarah is so happy to have Karen as her mom, and she adores her,"

Paul says. "She loves to snuggle with me, but she really connects with Karen, and I love that!"

"She loves to watch us dance together," Karen says. "It's the little-girl Cinderella romance thing, I think. But as far as she knows, kissing is still 'gross.' But she's okay with us giving each other a little peck. She sees how special our relationship is, and she appreciates it."

As Sarah enters puberty and starts asking questions, Karen is taking the lead on sex education. "Sarah is twelve now, so she's been asking questions for a while," Karen says. "We've had many talks, and she knows she can come to us and talk about what she's heard or seen. We want her to know the truth so she can make wise choices."

To enjoy some time alone, Karen and Paul will occasionally hire a babysitter or ask Grandma to visit so they can get away for a night and go to a hotel. "Sarah will complain, but we'll explain that Mommy and Daddy need some time alone to grow our love, and she's okay with that," Paul says. "She might not know what we're doing, but she understands we need alone time. No doubt, one day the realization will come to her and she'll say, 'Ewwww!'"

🌱 APPRAISING MY LIFE

Answer the following questions on your own. You may want to discuss some of these questions with your future mate when you discuss the "Assessing Our Lives" questions.

- How did you learn about sex?
- What experiences from your past might hinder healthy sex?
- Are you comfortable talking about sex?
- How have the media and culture influenced what you think about sex?
- What do you expect on your wedding night? What are your concerns?

- How comfortable are you with your body? Your appearance?
- How important is healthy sex to your partner and you?
- What about having more kids?
- What do you think about family planning? Contraception? Adoption?

🌱 ASSESSING OUR LIVES

Discuss the following questions together. Add any "Appraising My Life" questions you'd like to ask.

- Were you a victim of abuse in any way (sexual abuse, rape, incest, pornography, molestation, etc.)?
- If you were sexually active in the past, have you been tested for STDs or other problems?
- On a scale of one to five, how important is sex to you?
- How will your partner know if you want sex or just closeness?
- What worries do you have about sex?
- How often would you like to have sex?
- Can you both initiate sex?
- What is your attitude about giving or receiving sexual pleasure?
- What are your limits with sexual activity? Are there acts that aren't okay with you?
- What would ruin sexual intimacy for you?
- What would make sex really good for you?

🌱 A MOMENT FOR FUN!

What characteristic do you most want in a friend?

What's your favorite flavor of ice cream?

✿ APPLYING GOD'S WORD

God has a lot to say about sex and the purposes He has for sexual intimacy:

Sex is for recreation:

Enjoy life with your wife, whom you love, all the days of this mean-
ingless life that God have given you under the sun. (Ecclesiastes 9:9)

How delightful is your love, my sister, my bride! How much more
pleasing is your love than wine. (Song of Songs 4:10)

Sex is for communication:

The LORD God said, "It is not good for the man to be alone. I will
make a helper suitable for him." (Genesis 2:18)

Sex is for enjoying true intimacy:

For this reason a man will leave his father and mother and be united
to his wife, and they will become one flesh. (Genesis 2:24)

May your fountain be blessed, and may you rejoice in the wife of
your youth. A loving doe, a graceful deer—may her breasts satisfy you
always, may you ever be captivated by her love. (Proverbs 5:18–19)

Sex is for companionship:

If a man has recently married, he must not be sent to war or have any
other duty laid on him. For one year he is to be free to stay at home
and bring happiness to the wife he has married. (Deuteronomy 24:5)

Let us go early to the vineyards to see if the vines have budded, if their
blossoms have opened, and if the pomegranates are in bloom—there I
will give you my love. (Song of Songs 7:12)

Sex is to be pure:

> Blessed are the pure in heart, for they will see God. (Matthew 5:8)

> [Older women] can train the younger women to love their husbands and children, to be self-controlled and pure . . . so that no one will malign the word of God. (Titus 2:4–5)

> Marriage should be honored by all, and the marriage bed kept pure, for God will judge the adulterer and all the sexually immoral. (Hebrews 13:4)

Sex is for pleasure:

> The husband should fulfill his marital duty to his wife, and likewise the wife to her husband. The wife's body does not belong to her alone but also to her husband. In the same way, the husband's body does not belong to him alone but also to his wife. (1 Corinthians 7:3–4)

Sex is for procreation:

> So God created man in his own image, in the image of God he created him; male and female he created them. God blessed them and said to them, "Be fruitful and increase in number." (Genesis 1:27–28)

> Sons are a heritage from the LORD, children a reward from him. Like arrows in the hands of a warrior are sons born in one's youth. Blessed is the man whose quiver is full of them. (Psalm 127:3–5)

After you're married, read the book of Song of Songs together. It's a beautiful story of love, passion, and intimacy.

10

It's a Family Affair

What about Extended-Family Relationships?

It's safe to say that second marriages, especially with children, need the support, love, and encouragement that extended families can uniquely provide. The support Dale and I (Susan) experienced when we married was a beautiful thing. Sure, there were a couple of acquaintances who questioned the validity of remarriage, and one of our children wasn't too thrilled about the marriage, but overall, our children and extended families welcomed us with open arms. My mom was thrilled and happily welcomed Dale as her son; my siblings and some of my nieces and nephews came from the East Coast to attend our wedding. All five of our children became our wedding party. It was a great start to a wonderful life together.

The family history and the sense of community, continuity, and identity that extended families can bring to a newly blending family can be a strong and stabilizing force. While in-laws and extended-family relationships might also bring some relational challenges, they don't have to affect your marriage in a negative way. When you encounter an extended-family conflict, it's wise to discuss and deal with it together as a couple and figure out how to settle the issue as a team.

Tina and Karl discovered this reality early in their marriage. Both had lost their first spouses to cancer, and several years later, mutual friends introduced them. From the very beginning, Tina and Karl knew that there were big differences between their extended families, and although they didn't know how those differences might affect their relationship, they did their best to be proactive and plan for making their new little family a priority.

Tina and Karl saw the need to build a "solid partnership of honesty, openness, healthy communication, and faith in God," as Karl puts it. With this as their foundation, they strongly believed they could deal with whatever came their way.

"When we were dating," Tina says, "we'd write letters to each other, and we still have them. We talked about all kinds of things, from raising my five-year-old daughter, Jennie, to our strong faith, to the challenges that our extended families might bring, to what it would be like to live life on a large and remote ranch." After several months of intentional dating, Tina and Karl decided to marry and become a blended family.

Adjusting to Extended-Family Life

When Tina and Karl married, she was a city girl from a small family. He owned and operated a very large ranch far from even a small town.

"I feared I'd have mall withdrawal," Tina says. "But with such a large family and the busyness of the ranch, we looked forward to a little peace and quiet more often than not."

"There were adjustments, of course," Karl admits. "But for me, it was thrilling to have not only a wonderful wife but also a beautiful daughter. For Tina, the biggest adjustment was dealing with my very large extended family."

Though Tina's in-laws were loving and godly people, Tina and her daughter had never experienced such a close-knit family with a strong sense of community. This presented a significant challenge for Tina and Jennie.

"Still, the family embraced us both," Tina says, "and the grandparents spoiled Jennie, loved her completely, and cheered Jennie on in all she did."

Fortunately, Tina and Karl realized early on that the size and closeness of his extended family might hinder them from blending well. They decided to be proactive about making time for just the two of them and Jennie. So on the way home from their honeymoon, Tina and Karl actually bought a tent and some camping equipment to intentionally use with their new family—apart from the extended family. For years after that, they camped and traveled, building their relationships and just having fun together. Even today, both Tina and Karl believe that camping was an important part of keeping their little family strong and close.

Extended-Family Expectations

Yet even with Tina and Karl's proactive planning, unexpected surprises came their way. Since Karl's parents lived just yards from Tina and Karl's house, the extended family would come and have all-family get-togethers regularly, especially during the holidays. Then later, when Karl's mother got sick with cancer, the extended family came to visit her often.

"I'd often be cooking for up to thirty-five people for several days in a row," Tina says. "I really didn't know what was expected of me in the beginning. I came from a small family, so this was quite different and required some big adjustments on my part. The tradition of Karl hosting Christmas at his house was well established before I came, so I did my best to please Karl and his family.

"But after Karl's parents were deceased, I wrote a kind but firm letter to the rest of the family, suggesting that we establish 'creative Christmases' and go to the mountains or rotate host homes. We needed to establish a new boundary with our extended family, and though it was awkward at first, the family accepted this change and all ended well."

Such unforeseen expectations can be daunting, especially when a prior family was established in the extended-family circle. The new wife or husband and his or her kids might be a bigger adjustment for the extended family than many second-marriage couples realize.

Many in-laws try hard to love their new son- or daughter-in-law as well as support the couple, and most try to have respectful and healthy boundaries. When there are children involved, in-laws usually love and accept the stepchildren unconditionally. Yes, a few in-laws struggle to accept the new spouse and stepchildren, especially when they were close to the first spouse. And because the in-laws' lives, family traditions, and expectations are almost always different from those of the blending family, challenges—and sometimes conflict—will likely arise. When that happens, it's important to work together as a couple to discuss these situations and resolve any problems.

Extended-family dynamics can also influence a nuclear family in surprising and unexpected ways. Discuss as much as you can about these dynamics before you marry so you can alleviate as many misunderstandings as possible, but know that there will always be surprises along the way.

Since Karl was used to being an uncle to three small nephews who needed strong discipline at times, shortly after he and Tina were married, Karl made the mistake of giving Jennie a swat on her bottom when she disobeyed him. It was a quick and impulsive decision that he still regrets.

"She wasn't one of my wild little nephews who needed that," Karl says. "A simple word would've been sufficient. I was wrong, and it still haunts me."

"Jennie was crushed," Tina says. "She absolutely loved Karl to death, so it took her a long time to get over it. But we learned some important things from it that I wish we had known and discussed earlier. As the biological parent, I realized that I needed to take the total role of disciplining

Resolving Conflict and Setting Boundaries with Family Members, Parents, and In-Laws

1. Remember that your marriage relationship comes first, even if your family members, parents, or in-laws have a valid concern about a situation. Your spouse takes priority. That said, be sure to remain humble and as objective as possible. Be honest about your feelings and determine to resolve the situation.

2. Remember to be respectful when you talk about each other's families. Talk privately as a couple about the situation. Openly communicate and fairly resolve it together (see chapters 5 and 6). Then come to an agreement on how you'll handle the situation with your family members.

3. Go to your biological family together, or if needed, talk to them alone. During the discussion, be sure to protect your spouse and children. Realize that you're probably not going to change your family members' opinions, but assure them of your love and respect. Be calm and kind, but be clear and firm in the decision you made as a couple. Be sure your family understands that the two of you are in agreement, that you support your spouse, and that your marriage comes first.

4. Set clear boundaries with your extended family. Explain your rationale clearly and as objectively as possible. But do what's best for your marriage and your blending family. Remember that you can't please everyone all the time.

5. Love one another, regardless of the outcome. Ephesians 4:2 says, "Be completely humble and gentle; be patient, bearing with one another in love."

my daughter, while Karl needed to focus his role on simply loving and caring for her."

"Early in our marriage, we spent lots of time talking about all the lessons we learned and making the adjustments we needed to make," Karl says.

Dealing with Challenges

Tina and Karl realized that blending a family and having a successful second marriage needed a large dose of godly wisdom. So they sought to build that into their marriage.

"From the very beginning, prayer and spiritual growth were so important to us," Karl says. "When times got tough, when challenges came, we banded together spiritually. We often chose a day to fast for one meal. We talked and prayed not only about our personal issues but also about the needs of those around us.

"We'd both been through so much before we married that the tough things we faced after we married seemed kind of small and manageable. But we always knew we needed God's help with blending our family. Even now, when there's a problem or conflict, I can't let things build up and get out of hand. I go to Tina, and we talk things over—and we talk to God too."

"When Jennie was young and inquisitive, we'd often go into the laundry room and turn on the dryer so we could resolve our differences beyond her earshot," Tina says. "You do what you've got to do. I never wanted her to be in the middle of conflict."

Tina and Karl felt that any "discussions"—especially regarding the extended-family and in-law challenges—should be kept from Jennie's hearing, and that was wise. Because they'd built a firm foundation of talking about things honestly and openly as well as praying together, Tina and Karl were able to work through the extended-family challenges that came their way.

Family Differences

Though Tina's extended family was smaller and less involved in their daily lives, they nevertheless showed that they cared for this new family. In the midst of doing life, Karl and Tina's extended families also presented a few challenges.

Until Tina married Karl, her parents were very involved in Tina and Jennie's lives, and though her parents weren't Christians, they were kind and loving people. Grandpa would babysit, and Grandma would play with Jennie for hours.

As is often the case, Tina's family came around most when Jennie and Tina were hurting. And because strong bonds are forged through tough times, it is sometimes hard to adjust to the changes that come with a second marriage.

Shortly after Tina married, her parents moved to Texas for work, so their relationship with Tina and Jennie changed. Before the days of Skype and e-mail, it was a little harder to stay connected. They had to keep in touch by phone and letters.

Though the family dynamic changed with distance, everyone adjusted. During phone calls, Grandpa encouraged Jennie in math and science, while Grandma encouraged her granddaughter in her music and other endeavors. The distance made their interactions different but nonetheless important.

The reality is that in-law interactions can vary greatly. One set of in-laws may not want things to change—they may not want you to remarry, and they may put pressure on you to keep things as they are. Another set of in-laws may be all for the new marriage. One set of parents may be hands off and unengaged with your blending family, so they just go with whatever decisions you make. The other set may want to control, protect, and constantly give input—wanted or not. Or they may be detached and seemingly uncaring. Sometimes you even have to deal with in-law envy, especially when it comes to sharing relationships with grandchildren. Though none of these issues need to be a source of unsolvable conflict, deciding how your parents might respond to your second marriage might help you plan for the future.

Misunderstandings and Adjustments

In the midst of doing life, you and your extended families will undoubtedly experience misunderstandings, hurt feelings, fears, strained communication, or unreasonable expectations at times. That's just how relationships are. But hopefully those times will be few, and with good communication between you and your spouse, they don't have to affect your relationship negatively.

You and your future in-laws will probably deal with a few communication issues, now or later. You may experience some stress as they adjust to your new family, or they may have negative attitudes about how you live. They may even disagree with your beliefs, family traditions, child-rearing methods, and more. They may have expectations about holidays, family gatherings, blending-family issues, or responsibility for aging parents. But these issues can all be navigated successfully if you work together, first as a couple and then as a family. Instead of fearing the challenges that may come, instead, like Tina and Karl, embrace them as ways to learn more about your in-laws and opportunities to love them for who they are.

Unexpected situations will also come up with extended family. Just six months after Karl and Tina married, Karl's aging parents got sick and found that they could no longer physically care for Karl's disabled brother, who had cerebral palsy. So after much discussion and prayer, Tina and Karl brought him to live with them. Talk about challenges to a new marriage and a blending family!

The reality is that attitude is everything, and Tina tackled this challenge with the right attitude. "I've been pushing wheelchairs since I married

Karl," Tina says with a smile. "Though it's not what I expected, it's what God allowed."

When it came to extended-family relationships and the life circumstances that arose, Tina chose to have a genuinely positive attitude. In so doing, she became a successful and vital part of Karl's family. She also set a fine example for others to emulate.

Karl loved her for it. The extended family respected her, and her daughter, Jennie, learned how to give, serve, and share. It was a win-win for all of them.

Here are six ways to develop good relationships with your future in-laws and extended families:

1. *Openly discuss both of your families and learn all you can about them.* Though there will always be surprises, they should be limited if you take time to talk through your family intricacies. What differences might there be between you as a couple and your in-laws? Within limits, discuss what the positives—and negatives—are concerning each family member. How might each person impact your second marriage? How will your new spouse's extended family feel about your children, and what concerns might you have about your spouse's family accepting and fully embracing the kids?

As you talk, be careful not to be defensive or judgmental; simply be truthful and real. Do your families have different customs, faiths, moral beliefs, or traditions? Are there financial challenges, legal issues, health problems, or aging issues that need to be discussed? Are there family dysfunctions, such as physical, emotional, or alcohol abuse, that you'll need to set boundaries for and protect your family from? Are there childrearing attitudes that differ from yours? Discuss these possibilities and make a plan of action before you get in the middle of it.

Remember that your loyalty should be to your future spouse, and you should always stand united in whatever position you take. Finally, remember that no family is perfect, so don't take offense or take things too seriously. Give grace to your extended families and future in-laws, and follow Romans 12:18: "If it is possible, as far as it depends on you, live at peace with everyone."

2. Build relationships with your future in-laws. If you can, meet your future in-laws before the wedding. Go to their homes, if possible, so you can see how they live, and learn all you can about them. Let them meet your children. E-mail, Skype, text—talk! What do they love about your future spouse? Ask them. What common ground can you share together? Find out. Be respectful of their thoughts and ideas regarding the wedding—and beyond—even if you don't agree with them. If it's tough to connect or hard to relate, be polite and kind, regardless. Consider their input, but ultimately do what's best for your blending family.

3. Form your new family first. Often the expectations of in-laws and the couple differ, and that's a recipe for conflict. Set priorities and boundaries when you know what family dynamics might negatively affect your marriage relationship. Tina and Karl did what they could, yet they still found that blending their family was an ongoing and ever-changing journey. Though you may never figure out all the possible implications of extended-family relationships, be as proactive as possible.

4. Consider the holidays. Especially with blending-family situations, children may be expected to go here, there, and everywhere during the holidays—to celebrate with both sets of biological parents *and* participate in extended-family celebrations as well as in blending-family gatherings. Plan ahead—way ahead—to alleviate the potential for offense, hurt, misunderstanding, and frustration. All the individuals involved might have unrealistic expectations, so take the time to work on your holiday plans as a couple first and then as a blending family. Discuss which holidays are most important to you, which family traditions you want to carry into your new family, what new traditions you want to form, and what visitation situations are necessary. Then make plans accordingly.

Because holidays can get so complicated, give adequate attention to making plans that are best for your blending family first, and then carefully consider the rest of the clan. Some couples even plan two to five years out so that everyone can look forward to a rotation of family time together, as well as manage the expenses those visits might incur. Once you decide as a couple, communicate your decisions to everyone involved.

5. *Establish boundaries early.* Though Tina and Karl's extended families were good-hearted, loving, and kind, they still brought stress and required Tina and Karl to set boundaries. When setting boundaries with your extended families, try to emphasize the best of each family situation and honor your future in-laws. Avoid being critical or judgmental when things get tough. How will you handle visits, get-togethers, and gift giving? What expectations might your extended family have of you as a couple?

Be sure you and your future spouse don't keep any secrets between the two of you, and don't share negative information about your future mate with your family members. Ask your parents to call before coming to visit, and if boundaries are broken, reestablish them together as a couple. When there are differences in childrearing or other situations with the children, work together to resolve the issues, and be sure the children aren't caught in the middle of the disagreement or feel torn between families. And when there are differences, remember that your future spouse and children must come first.

6. *When conflict happens, be careful.* Conflicts will arise with extended family, but remember to "do to others what you would have them do to you" (Matthew 7:12). Be grace-filled and merciful, get on the same page as your future mate, and let your partner take the lead in resolving conflict with his or her family members. With in-laws, remember to "honor your father and mother" (Ephesians 6:2). With siblings or other extended-family members, discuss the situations and plan accordingly. Forming your new family while adjusting to relationships with in-laws and extended family can be daunting, but it can also be one of the best aspects of your life together. Extended-family life can give you a wonderful

heritage, a rich group of friends, a place to learn new things, and an amazing family life—if you choose to enjoy the journey.

☙ BLENDING WITH KIDS

What about the Previous Extended Family?

When you have children, it's important to help them stay connected to the other biological parent's family. Too often, second marriages result in broken extended-family relationships, and this will hurt the children. They are forever connected to that biological extended family, for better or for worse. They are related by blood and by heritage, whether or not you are married to their biological parent. Neither death nor divorce can change that reality.

Unless it's an abusive or unsafe situation, your children need relationships with both sides of grandparents and extended families, even when they are the "ex" family to you or that biological parent is no longer alive.

Why is this important?

- Because your children need to stay connected to their blood relatives, learn about their heritage, and feel a part of their relatives' lives.
- Because your children need the reassurance that family goes on, even when there's a divorce or death. They need to know that family matters, and that family is there for life.
- Because your children need family members to encourage them, support them, and cheer them on as they grow and mature, whether it's at a school play, a recital, or a sports event, or later when it's time for college, marriage, or a career.
- Because your children need to know it's okay to have relationships with the other family members without fearing that you'll be bothered by it. They need to know you love them enough to let them share that biological bond.

- Because they already share a special bond with these family members and don't need another "divorce" or "death" by being separated from them.

Better yet, gaining the support of grandparents and step-grandparents will greatly benefit your children by giving them continuity, love, and the reassurance that they need. Grandparents and step-grandparents can also play an important role in helping your children adjust to a blending family, if they are all made to feel accepted and comfortable in their roles. Demonstrate your acceptance of grandparents and step-grandparents. Invite them to participate in your family life. Help them navigate the relationships by clearly defining your needs and expectations.

How can you do this?

- Reassure grandparents and step-grandparents that you want them to have relationships with the grandchildren, and encourage them to continue the relationships as before.

- Plan events so new step-grandparents can get to know the children, and let them know that there's no "step" in grandparenting as far as you're concerned.

- Encourage your children to call, visit, write, e-mail, and Skype with family members, especially all the grandparents, regularly. Whether it's a weekly or monthly contact, make it a regular and special event.

- Share events in your children's lives with all the grandparents, such as science fairs, school fund-raisers, great report cards, and so on.

- Invite grandparents and step-grandparents to your children's ball games, recitals, honor celebrations, graduations, and so on.

- Take pictures and share them regularly with all the grandparents.

- Include all the grandparents in holiday giving, even if it's just a simple Christmas card.

- Acknowledge each grandparent's and step-grandparent's birthday or other special occasions.

Grandparents, step-grandparents, and extended family from all sides can give your children love and support like no one else can, and the lasting rewards will be great. This network of loving adults can be an important part of the second-marriage and blending-family journey.

APPRAISING MY LIFE

Map out your family tree as far as you can. If you have children, do a separate tree for the other parent's family. Add one or two words to describe how you experienced each person (successful businessman, alcoholic, funny, grumpy, faithful, manipulative, kind, etc.). Jot down some notes about your family history and discuss these with your future mate.

Answer the following questions, and then talk about them with your future spouse:

- Are you too involved with or too disconnected from your parents or extended family?
- Are you concerned that your future spouse is too close to or distant from his or her parents or extended family?
- Are you comfortable with your future in-laws? What concerns do you have?

ASSESSING OUR LIVES

Discuss your families together, especially in relation to your children:

- What do you like and dislike about your parents? Your extended family? Your former spouse's family (if you have children)?
- Are there family secrets, unhealthy patterns, dysfunctions, or other challenges in your family?
- What concerns do you have about your future in-laws?
- Are you worried about interfering in-laws? What is the concern, and what will you do as a couple when problems arise?

- What are your families' expectations regarding your relationship?
- What are your expectations as a couple regarding how your relationships with your families might change?
- Will your families expect to see you regularly? How often?
- What boundaries do you need to set, especially regarding the children?
- What will you do about holidays?
- What family traditions and customs would you like to continue?

☘ A MOMENT FOR FUN!

What age was the best time of your life so far?

Imagine you could hold one position in government. What would it be?

☘ APPLYING GOD'S WORD

Here are some important scriptures to consider when relating to in-laws and extended family:

Cursed is the man who dishonors his father or his mother. (Deuteronomy 27:16)

If a man curses his father or mother, his lamp will be snuffed out in pitch darkness. (Proverbs 20:20)

Blessed are the peacemakers, for they will be called sons of God.
(Matthew 5:9)

Do nothing out of selfish ambition or vain conceit, but in humility
consider others better than yourselves. Each of you should look
not only to your own interests, but also to the interests of others.
(Philippians 2:3–4)

Get rid of all bitterness, rage and anger, brawling and slander, along
with every form of malice. Be kind and compassionate to one another,
forgiving each other, just as in Christ God forgave you. (Ephesians
4:31–32)

Whatever is true, whatever is noble, whatever is right, whatever is
pure, whatever is lovely, whatever is admirable—if anything is excellent
or praiseworthy—think about such things. (Philippians 4:8)

Make every effort to live in peace with all men and to be holy; without
holiness no one will see the Lord. See to it that no one misses the grace
of God and that no bitter root grows up to cause trouble and defile
many. (Hebrews 12:14–15)

11

Time for Teamwork

*How Do You Handle
the Nitty-Gritty of Daily Life?*

It's a fact that every moment of every day you're expected to fulfill certain roles and responsibilities and make hundreds of decisions, large and small. It's the stuff of daily life that can make you crazy! But your attitude about each day makes all the difference in the world.

Dale and I (Susan) see our commitment to teamwork as a great asset in accomplishing the stuff of daily life. In fact, we've found that maintaining an attitude that puts the team (us as a couple) ahead of personal desires really helps us accomplish much more than we could if we were more concerned about what's fair and right for *me* as an individual.

We do just about everything together. I cook and Dale cleans up. We pitch in and do the chores—inside and out. When one of us sees something that needs doing, we just do it, regardless of whose regular job it tends to be. If there's an errand to run, one of us does it regardless of whether it's convenient or not.

Yes, there are times when one of us is busy or sick or tired, and the other has to pick up the slack for a while. But we try to remain flexible—I know there's nothing Dale wouldn't do for me, and vice versa. Decisions, chores, and the stuff of daily life are, after all, just stuff.

Because there are so many ways to go about making daily decisions, we're going to let three very different couples share about this topic instead of just one. Let's meet them.

Alyson and Brice

Alyson had a four-year-old little boy, Robbie, when she married Brice, and now they also have a son together, Ryan. Robbie is bipolar and has an attachment disorder, so they face some extra challenges daily.

"God meant for us to be together and to be a family," Alyson says. "Although we have our struggles with Robbie, we're in this for the long haul."

"Leaving the single lifestyle to be a husband and stepdad was something I was ready to do," Brice says. "And although blending a family isn't always easy, being Robbie's stepdad is a good thing."

Sharon and Zach

Sharon was a widowed, single mother of a seventeen-year-old girl, Cara, when she married Zach, who had a twelve-year-old girl, Rachel. For the first several months of Zach and Sharon's marriage, both girls lived with them.

"When we were first married, we drew up our family covenant and family rules and had a family meeting," Sharon says. "One of the most important family rules was to respect each other."

"I could sense the tension," Zach says. "We talked everything out—our expectations, dreams, frustrations, and the good things about our new family. We then put up a wedding picture of the four of us as a sign of establishing us as a family. I think it helped get us on the same page."

Jill and Nick

Jill and Nick met when their kids were very young, so they took a few years to heal from their divorces and get to know each other well before they married. Jill's children are now ten and twelve; Nick's children are ten, thirteen, and fifteen. They have been blending their family for more than seven years.

"When you get married, you should spend a lot of time bonding as a couple," Jill says. "But you also have to help your kids adjust, and you have to try to bond with your stepkids. Sometimes it's not easy to juggle it all."

"In a second marriage you have to be very flexible," Nick says. "I'm not only marrying Jill; I'm marrying her kids. And I'm marrying her ex's schedule, and she's marrying my ex's schedule. And the schedule of her ex-husband's new wife affects us. So does her ex-in-laws' schedule, and so does the schedule of her ex-husband's new wife's kid! We might have something planned, but if her ex's wife's ex messes up the schedule, it flows right down to us!"

All three of these couples have different daily challenges, but they all realize that standing united and working together makes life more peaceful and productive. "We share the same goals," Jill says. "We stay on the same track, and that's half the battle."

First Things First

Dividing up the work is often one of the first challenges that newly remarried couples face. How do you get everything done in the limited time you have? Who does what chores? Who runs what errands? Who cares for the kids?

"We work as a team to get the cooking and the house stuff done, as well as getting the kids to their activities," Nick says. "Whatever needs to be done, we just do it."

So how do you figure out what roles each of you will assume, how you will delegate responsibilities, and how you will make decisions?

The three keys to success in this area are being unselfish, staying balanced, and making decisions appropriately. Who is best skilled to accomplish a particular task? Who has the time to run a certain errand? Find the balance so you avoid resentment, and share the workload so you accomplish life's everyday challenges together. Both are important for keeping stress at bay.

"Marriage is so much about working together and just getting it done," Zach says. "It's not about me; it's about us. When Sharon and I don't work together, things get out of whack."

Zach is right. Keeping score or demanding that everything be doled out fifty-fifty is ineffective and often counterproductive. Dale and I (Susan) have seen this mentality all too often with couples. We encourage you to decide now to simply work as a team to get things done. Life is too short to keep score and argue over whose job something is.

Wired to Work

Throughout this book we've stressed how God's redemptive plan for your second marriage can change life for the good, and that includes how you work out your roles and responsibilities. The decisions made in prior marriages, or a person's views about roles and responsibilities, may not quite align with how God has wired us.

The world's confusing views of male and female roles, especially in marriage, often influence us, consciously or unconsciously. For example, since the role of cooking always fell to me (Susan) in my first marriage, I could've sent the signal to my kids that cooking was a "woman's job." But my son has loved cooking since he was little, so I intentionally broke the role mold and encouraged that interest. He is now a successful manager of three restaurants!

It really doesn't matter what the traditional male or female roles might have been in the past. Be careful not to fall into roles just because it's always been that way. Simply use the gifts, talents, interests, and abilities you have to serve one another.

According to God's plan, you are here on this earth to love and serve. If that's the case, then your role as a husband or wife is primarily to love and serve your mate.

"Servant leadership is extremely important to me as a husband and a dad," Nick says. "This means that nothing is too big or too small to do. It may mean that I pitch in and help in the kitchen. It may mean that I take one of Jill's kids to soccer while she takes the other to music lessons. By serving her kids, I serve her!"

"In the busyness of family life, we serve each other in lots of little ways," Jill says. "Nick makes coffee every morning, holds the door for me, does the dishes, and all kinds of other stuff."

There are so many ways to serve each other—by meeting one another's needs, fulfilling each other's expectations, or being patient and loving toward the children and stepchildren. In the area of roles and meeting the responsibilities of daily life, God also created us uniquely by making us men and women.

Gender differences have been a hot-button issue for many years, but let's set aside our preconceived notions for a minute and think about how God really created us. If we can first gain a biblical view of our male and female roles, then we'll have a head start in making daily life peaceful and united in our blending families.

God made man to naturally be the protector, provider, and leader—and ultimately the one responsible for the family. Men are wired for this task, and if we as women will treat them that way and respect them for how God made them, things should work well (1 Corinthians 11:3).

"I love that Zach is the leader of our home," Sharon says. "It's one of the reasons I married him. He is so strong in his faith, and he brought that strength to our family."

God made woman to naturally be a helper, a completer, a nurturer, a balancer, and a life giver (Genesis 2:20–22). Together, you and your future spouse can accomplish so much more than you can apart. Do whatever is necessary to accomplish the tasks at hand, no matter what. That's what matters most. And men, as you work with your future mate on the household chores, she'll appreciate your efforts!

"Zach and I fell into doing the household chores in a pretty traditional way," Sharon says. "But when I can't get it all done right away, he does whatever he can to help."

"I like things orderly," Zach says. "When I make things neat and tidy, I'm in my element. I need things to be somewhat organized for my own comfort."

"I'm not as much of a perfectionist," Sharon says, "so finding balance is a work in progress for us."

Some couples struggle with this more than others. The point is to make life easier by having a servant's attitude about getting the job done, no matter who does what or how it gets done.

Daily Life with Your Man

As women, it's good to affirm the efforts our men make to provide for and protect us. Verbally affirm what your future husband does in accomplishing his responsibilities for you and your family, and he'll be a happy man indeed.

"To be honest, I sometimes get worn out in all the busyness of blending a family," Nick says. "But Jill affirms me regularly. She texts me and says, 'Thank you so much for all you do for our family. You're such a blessing to us, and we appreciate you.' I can be dead tired, and that energizes me so much!"

One of the best ways to meet your man's need for affirmation is to demonstrate it by the way you speak to him—with respect, love, and kindness. This is especially important when speaking to others about him.

Daily Life with Your Woman

God designed your wife to need protection, acceptance, support, understanding, sensitivity, and connection with you. God expects men to meet the needs of their wives. And vice versa.

"The time Alyson and I spend together is really important," Brice says. "We enjoy horseback riding, boating, and other things. And we've always set aside date nights. We are united, and whether we're working the business together, raising the kids, or spending time with family or friends, we do it together, and we make time for fun."

Patience and understanding go a long way toward making your relationship with your wife loving, intimate, and fulfilling for you both. Yet commitment is probably the most important thing to a woman. She needs reassurance that you are in the relationship for life. She needs assurance that your loyalty, devotion, and fidelity are steadfast.

Balancing One Another

In this discussion we've seen that God has given the responsibility to the husband to be the leader and has wired the wife to help him be successful in family life. A man's and a woman's roles are unique, but they're also equal in value in God's eyes.

"Brice and I are equal, but we have our different roles, and I'm okay with that," Alyson says. "I love that Brice supports my desire to stay home with the kids. I am happy to be a homemaker and nurturer. And I love that he's such a strong and loyal provider and protector."

To understand this balance, here's a great metaphor Susan and I (Dale) heard: Marriage is like a tandem bike. The lead rider and the co-rider are on the same level, working together for a common goal as they stay in sync with each other. They pedal toward the same destination, but the leader steers the bike, provides the steady pace, protects them from potential danger, and works with his co-rider to reach their destination. They must stay balanced or they'll fall. They must stay in sync and connected as a team or they'll crash. They must communicate and adjust to one another or they'll have problems.

You can bring balance to your daily life in many ways: by being strong when the other is weak; by being the nurturer when the other has to be the disciplinarian; by picking up the slack when the other is weary; by supporting each other in your jobs, in parenting, in friendships, in ministry. The bottom line is this: "In everything, do to others what you would have them do to you" (Matthew 7:12).

Be-Attitudes of Daily Living

So how do you make teamwork happen? How do you get the daily work done, complete those mundane duties, and accomplish chores in the midst of blending a family—all while staying in harmony with one another? It's all about attitude!

"Keeping a good attitude while in the stress of life is so much about keeping God first," Jill says. "God gives you the joy, peace, and strength—you get those things by reading the Bible every day. I could be mad that Nick has to drive ten to twelve hours every other weekend to see his kids, but I choose to have a good attitude and support him in his responsibilities. God helps me do that."

Here are eight be-attitudes that any couple can use to make everyday decisions, duties, and jobs a breeze:

1. Be positive. Determine what's most important and why. Don't sweat the small stuff. Tackle the mundane with a positive attitude and enthusiasm.
2. Be unselfish. Pull your own weight. Don't expect your partner to do all—or even most—of the work. Do your fair share and don't keep score if you feel you're pulling more of the load at times.
3. Be willing to use your skills and abilities. Use your strengths. If he's a good cook and she's a good mechanic, go for it. Don't feel tied to traditional duties; use each other's skills to your mutual benefit.
4. Be a team. Take on work as a team or "divide and conquer." Just be sure to choose duties together and compromise peacefully when necessary.
5. Be servants. Just as Jesus washed His disciples' feet, serve each other—by doing a chore without the other knowing it or by making dinner when the other has had a tough day.
6. Be content. You know that there are always things to be done, but avoid becoming discontent and grumbling. Chores are a part of life.
7. Be adaptable to change. When one of you is sick or working extra hours, the other should pick up the slack for a while.
8. Be careful to use time management. It's always easy to put off those mundane tasks, but they'll just pile up and get worse. Manage your time so you can deal with chores on a daily or weekly basis; this will keep your family life running more smoothly.

Decisions, Decisions

Part of married life is making those many decisions you're faced with each and every day. Whether it's about finances, time management, or making love, how do you make all those decisions? And who gets the final say in a decision that's hard to resolve?

"Jill and I make most of our decisions together," Nick says, "but when there's a stalemate, it gets challenging. We have a combined set of family rules, but when it's a decision about my children, I'll listen to all the input, but ultimately, I'll make the decisions about my kids. And Jill does the same with hers."

"If Nick and I argue about anything, it usually has to do with the exes," Jill says. "When situations with our exes affect us and the kids, it gets even harder. But ultimately, it's my decision how I deal with my ex, and Nick's with his ex."

There are also major and minor decisions that need to be made on a regular basis. Each decision should be given the amount (a little or a lot) of weight and time it deserves. There are scary decisions, such as whether to have elective surgery, and there are times when there is a stalemate in the decision-making process.

"Recently my alcoholic father came to stay with us for a while," Alyson says, "and that was tough. It's hard for me to say no to my family."

"It can be stressful deciding when and how to set boundaries with family members, especially with my father-in-law," Brice says. "I finally had to say, 'We can't be a bed-and-breakfast anymore.'"

"I know I need to get better at setting boundaries," Alyson says. "These kinds of things can tear a couple apart if you don't work them out."

No matter how big or small the decisions are, as a couple you should try your best to come to a mutual agreement on them. To do all this, you must use your communication skills, cooperate, and often compromise, all the while respecting each other's values, goals, and dreams.

"In the middle of making any kind of decision, Zach will stop and pray about it," Sharon says.

"We need to seek God in everything and be willing to obey Him," Zach says.

It's wise to pray together, especially before you make big decisions, and then submit them to God and His Word. Priorities should align with God's priorities for your life—God, spouse, family, and work . . . in that order. And your priorities as a couple should be compatible.

"Balancing everyday life is a constant challenge," Nick says. "I've had to cut back on a lot of things during this season of our family life, and that's okay. I know it's just a season."

"I talk with the kids to help them decide what's important and what's realistic," Jill says. "Can we really fit one more activity into the schedule? I also put clear boundaries on activities—if grades drop, then an activity drops off the schedule."

As you address the roles, responsibilities, duties, and decisions of daily life in your blending family, work together as a team to get the tasks, chores, and jobs done in a fair, appropriate, and unselfish manner. This will make your daily life more peaceful, pleasant, and productive.

🌿 BLENDING WITH KIDS

How Do We Manage Daily Life in a Blending Family?
Chores. School. Homework. Extracurricular activities. Friends. Church. Whew! And what about noncustodial kids who come every other weekend, on holidays, or only in the summer? Daily life for a newly remarried couple with a child or two can get very complicated, and it can wear you out in a hurry. What do you do?

"Before we married, we talked a lot about how we were going to parent," Brice says, "but you never really know until you're in the middle of it. Parenting takes a lot of communicating, being patient and compassionate, and dealing with things as a team. Even making decisions about chores, school, consequences, and all those sorts of things takes a lot of work."

"I'm so thankful that Brice has stepped up and been the dad that Robbie never would have had," Alyson says. "With Robbie's attachment disorder, it's hard for him to connect. He struggles with denial, lying, and not being sorry for the wrong things he does, so daily life is a challenge for us."

"Robbie calls me 'Dad,' and I love that," Brice says. "For all we face with Robbie, one day he'll look back and realize that I didn't *have* to be involved; I *wanted* to be involved."

"Parenting Robbie has definitely been the toughest part of our marriage," Alyson says, "and though it's not an easy journey, I'm glad we're doing it together."

Alyson is right! More often than not, parenting and stepparenting in a blending family can be the toughest part of your marriage. But it can also be a place where God can work on healing broken hearts and lives, growing children who will become healthy and productive adults, and guiding you together as a couple to make your daily life one of peace and harmony.

Projecting a united front is key. Setting boundaries is often critical. And balancing each other is important.

"Just before we got married, I overheard my stepdaughter, Rachel, say, 'Oh, good, now I have someone to do my laundry,'" Sharon says. "She expected me to take over and do everything for her."

"Sometimes it's hard for me to see the bigger picture," Zach says. "I see the smaller issue of the moment, but Sharon helps me see how that issue can affect Rachel's future."

"We try to balance each other, but sometimes it's not easy," Sharon says.

Balancing custodial and noncustodial kids and all their roles, responsibilities, and schedules can also be daunting. It's important to communicate clearly and often.

"We coordinate our kids' schedules so that we have time alone as a couple," Jill says. "Especially in those first few years, it's critical to have time together without the stress of the kids. If we need to, we'll utilize family and friends so we can keep our marriage strong."

"When my sons are with us, they're expected to abide by the household rules and be part of the family routine," Nick says. "So they go to the soccer games to support their brother and sister, or whatever. And in the summer, they have their own chores and are a part of the regular family routine."

"When there are different rules in the other home, it can be tough for kids," Jill says. "But it's amazing how quickly they adjust, so we don't worry about it so much anymore."

Managing blending-family daily life can be overwhelming, but with patience and lots of communication, it can be done.

"Take one day at a time and enjoy every moment with your spouse and kids," Jill says. "Life goes by so fast."

🌿 APPRAISING MY LIFE

Think about each of the following questions, and then discuss them with your future mate.

- What were your previous marriage roles? What would you like to keep, give up, or change?
- What does leadership in the home look like to you? Why?
- What would you like your roles to look like as a married couple?
- Why are affirmation and attitude important?
- How will you make decisions, especially about the kids?
- How can you balance each other?

🌿 ASSESSING OUR LIVES

Discuss God's roles for men and women with your future mate; then answer the following questions.

- What gifts and talents do each of you bring to the family?
- What do these words mean to you: *service, respect, honor, appreciation, trust,* and *teamwork*?

- How will you decide who does what? Do you have an equal vote? How will you compromise?
- Who will be in charge of finances?
- How will you make decisions about buying large-ticket items, such as a house or a car?
- How will you decide what church to attend?
- Who will decide when you will spend time with friends or family? What about how you spend free time (vacations, hobbies, sports, etc.)?
- Who will stay home with the children, or will you use childcare?
- How will you discipline and make decisions about the children?

❦ A MOMENT FOR FUN!

Who's the most compassionate person you've ever met?

Imagine you could move your workplace anyplace in the world. Where would you go?

❦ APPLYING GOD'S WORD

Read the following scriptures and discuss how they relate to everyday life in a second marriage:

I have set you an example that you should do as I have done for you. I tell you the truth, no servant is greater than his master, nor is a messenger greater than the one who sent him. (John 13:15–16)

Be imitators of God, therefore, as dearly loved children and live a life
of love, just as Christ loved us and gave himself up for us as a fragrant
offering and sacrifice to God. (Ephesians 5:1–2)

Submit to one another out of reverence for Christ. (Ephesians 5:21)

Do nothing out of selfish ambition or vain conceit, but in humility
consider others better than yourselves. Each of you should look
not only to your own interests, but also to the interests of others.
(Philippians 2:3–4)

Husbands, in the same way be considerate as you live with your wives,
and treat them with respect . . . and as heirs with you of the gracious
gift of life, so that nothing will hinder your prayers. (1 Peter 3:7)

A Hope-Filled Journey

What about the Rest of Your Life Together?

Dale and I (Susan) have found this remarriage journey to be an adventure like none other. We thought that raising kids would be a joy and challenge, and it was. But seeing God work in our lives so beautifully through our marriage, blending-family stuff, health issues, work challenges, and so much more has been a blessing beyond measure.

So every year we celebrate our anniversary, sometimes by renewing our vows and always by rejoicing in our years together and remembering God's faithfulness. We look back on our years together, thanks to a shelf full of photo albums and lots of happy memories. And despite the fact that Dale has been diagnosed with Parkinson's disease, we choose to look ahead with faith, even while knowing that the disease will eventually progress and our days together will get more challenging. Yet we also know who holds our future—a faithful God who will be with us every step of the way.

We've covered a lot of territory in this book. We've talked about the importance of redemption and covenant, and we've discussed what the Bible has to say about how we communicate our love to each other. Now it's time to start the adventure by putting it all into practice.

"Trust the information and the affirmation you have received during your engagement period—from the books you've read, the prayers that have been answered, and the counsel you've received from those who love you as a couple," Tina and Karl say.

You've carefully assessed your personal life, and you've cautiously evaluated your relationship with your future spouse. And hopefully you've asked lots of questions and had many hours of talking together. You've learned tips and techniques on how to deal with needs and expectations, communication and conflict, money and sex, extended family and daily living—and about blending your family.

Megan and Tom give some pretty good universal advice: "Keep a good sense of humor through all your ups and downs. Always be open to growing, have a positive attitude, and maintain a godly perspective when things get rough."

As on any journey, there are often beautiful moments and wonderful surprises. This has certainly been true for us. There are times of love and laughter, joy and adventure. But there are also dangers, seen and unseen—road bumps, potholes, detours, hazards, and difficulties along the way. When you're on a journey, you inevitably learn new things and, hopefully, continue to grow. You enjoy new experiences, meet interesting people, and encounter new challenges. And when you begin this journey of blending a family, you'll experience all of these things—sometimes in just one day!

Dale and I (Susan) love to experience new adventures. Whether we're hiking in the Rocky Mountains, scrambling up the famous Dunn's River waterfall in Jamaica—just as a hurricane hit—or holding a wild baby lion cub in South Africa, we try to enjoy everything our journey has to offer.

That goes for our marriage as well. We enjoy the good times, make great memories, and capture the moments of fun and adventure. But when times get tough, when storms come, or when roadblocks hinder our path, we try to realize that the road bumps and potholes are just part of making an adventure unique. So we work together to overcome each obstacle that attempts to impede our journey.

Susan and I (Dale) have experienced medical challenges—cancer, Parkinson's disease, multiple surgeries, hospitalizations, and illnesses. We've had challenges in our adult children's lives—financial stresses, unemployment, school struggles, health issues, and major moves across the country and the world. We've had life challenges—job changes, aging parents, home and car repairs, and so much more. All these circumstances have actually brought us closer together because we've chosen to lean on each other, to draw strength from one another. You can do the same.

Sometimes your marriage will be easy, but other times the potholes or detours of life, the circumstances and the challenges that come your way, will test your marriage and your faith. Yet if you embrace the wisdom of God, He will lead you and guide you through the tough times. He will even carry you over those treacherous mountain passes and through the valleys of hard times . . . if you allow Him to.

Jennifer and Ben's first year of marriage presented lots of challenges. "The challenges we experienced drew us together rather than apart," they tell us. "There were a lot of things in our lives that were outside our control, and we just had to let the Lord take care of those things. We'd work with the things we could control, but that was limited. Dealing with the exes was tough at times, and kid stuff was definitely challenging. But we chose to deal with each situation as a team, and it made our second marriage strong."

Especially in the tough times, remember that your second marriage is so much bigger than just two people joining forces to journey through life together. It's even bigger than blending your family, although that is definitely *big*! It's about how you love each other God's way. Dale and I (Susan) make sure we keep this in mind as we make life decisions.

"Make sure God is the foundation of who you are individually, and then make God the center of your relationship," Karen and Paul say. "To keep your marriage strong, be sure to bring God into everything you do."

"Love people as they are, and let God do the rest," Megan and Tom say. "Accept your spouse—and his or her kids—for who they are, and don't hope to make any great changes. Instead of seeing things as annoying traits, think of those things as endearing qualities. If you keep God in the middle of your marriage and family, it'll be that much easier, because God's love is bigger than the love you can give."

If you allow it, your remarriage can be a special part of God's bigger story, for you have the privilege of showing others—including your children, family, friends, and community—what God intends for marriage. As you choose to intentionally develop your relationship in a godly way, and as you seize the moments to love deeply, treat each other respectfully, serve each other lavishly, and forgive completely, you'll find that the journey of remarriage can be the most exciting adventure you could ever experience. Dale and I (Susan) are continually amazed at how God uses our marriage—and the marriages of those you've read about—to show others His love for us.

Blending your family starts with making your marriage strong and then forming a family bond over time. One of our favorite songs about the beauty and intimacy of marriage is Steven Curtis Chapman's "Echoes of Eden." The song says, "These [times of intimacy and the relationship between a married couple] are the echoes of Eden, reflections of what we were created for. Hints of the passion and freedom [await] on the other side of heaven's door."[1] Your marriage relationship really can be an echo—a reflection—of God's redemption and how He created married life to be.

"But be cautious, because a second marriage is so much different from the first," Jill and Nick say. "It's not just 'chapter two'—everything is so much more complicated! You have your marriage, but you also have your kids—his, hers, and sometimes ours. So be teachable and open to learn all you can before you marry, and then be completely committed to each other."

Your Wedding

It's wise to keep your wedding day in perspective. If you want God to be a crucial part of your relationship, you can use your wedding to model a God-centered second marriage and the redemptive work He's doing in your lives.

Together Dale and I (Susan) spent quite a few hours preparing for our wedding, but we purposefully kept it simple and inexpensive. We had all five of our children in our wedding party, and because many of our family and friends were not Christians, we were careful to use this occasion as a gentle witness and a testimony of God's work in our lives.

You, too, can show others that you are making this covenant as an active, strategic choice to love each other through the seasons, changes, challenges, and joys of your marriage and blending-family journey. As you dedicate your second marriage to God during your wedding, you can reflect and honor Him and show your families and friends that the promises you are making today are sacred vows that will last as long as you both shall live.

"We made the theme of God's redemption the center of our wedding because He is our foundation," Linda and Rick say. "This second marriage is an example of God's loving-kindness and His grace in our lives, and it was our chance to love again, as Christ loved us. That's what we wanted to portray."

"We decided to say vows to our kids," Jill and Nick say. "Each of us vowed to raise the other's children as if they were our own. And we made a commitment to be a family, no matter what."

The Honeymoon

As with your wedding plans, we suggest you plan your honeymoon within your financial budget so you can focus on your relationship and not worry about going into debt. This should be a time for just the two of you—no matter how much you want to get on with blending your family.

Here are a few suggestions from the couples in this book about making your honeymoon special:

- Delay your honeymoon departure a day or two to recuperate locally.
- Keep travel arrangements simple.
- Rest during your honeymoon.
- Have fun as a couple.
- Don't talk too much about the kids; this is your time.
- Leave the kids at home!

New Beginnings

Your honeymoon season should last far beyond the honeymoon trip, and though that's more challenging when you have kids at home, you should intentionally plan for time alone as a couple on a weekly basis, especially during the first year of your marriage. You need this foundational time to really become one, build a solid team, and grow your roots deep as a couple.

Susan and I (Dale) intentionally formed lots of daily traditions that first year, and we set time aside to deepen our relationship. We also chose to spend time with our friends during the day so that we had our evenings alone together, and we chose not to get involved in too many activities outside the home.

Many of those traditions are still with us. Before we even get out of bed, we pray together for the day and for the needs around us. And nearly every evening, we give each other a back or foot rub while we pray before going to sleep. Be sure to find a few little traditions that will bind you together and create special and lasting couple time.

"Listen to the wisdom of other couples who are in second marriages, and follow their advice," Megan and Tom suggest. "People who have 'been there, done that' have wisdom you need."

Don't expect that everything will be perfect during this first season of your second-marriage adventure. When kids are involved, it's unrealistic to expect a really smooth transition. All of you—especially the children—may experience fear, awkwardness, disappointment, regret, discomfort, and conflict. That's not unusual when you're adjusting to any new adventure in life. Allow time for your relationships to grow and mature. And get help from others when you need it.

"Don't have unrealistic expectations that all will go perfectly," Isabel and Marcos say. "We guarantee that lots of adjustments will be needed during the first year of marriage so you can work out the 'ripples' that will be inevitably present."

You can build a healthy home and marriage right from the start by asking yourselves a few questions: What should our priorities be? How can we spend quality time together? What might each of us need to sacrifice now for the good of our family and for building a strong marriage? Don't let the distractions of this life get in the way of growing a healthy marriage.

"During the first year, focus as much as you can on building this new family unit," Tina and Karl say. "That might mean limiting outside commitments or maybe even working fewer hours. We desired to become a solid nuclear family early on, so we focused on making memories and building our family traditions. Sometimes it was even important for us to occasionally skip established patterns, like going to church or doing our favorite activities, in order to reconnect and bond as a family."

You might need to let go of some of your prior commitments or break some of the old habits and make new couple habits. Find ways to unite in your plans, purposes, decisions, and responsibilities of your marriage adventure. This will help you more easily adjust to the new journey you're on. Carefully decide what's important to building your relational growth, and get rid of things that are counterproductive to building a strong second marriage and blending your family well.

Now is a great time to start forming positive traditions that will continue your entire married life. There's no better way to grow closer as a couple than to learn to pray together regularly. Morning and evening chats can start and end your day with valuable communication. And just doing life together, whether it's running errands, working on the budget, cleaning the house, enjoying family and friends, or taking a walk, can help you establish positive traditions early in your married life.

"The first habit we established early in our marriage was having a morning quiet time together," Linda and Rick say. "We read Bible passages, and then we pray together. This builds a foundation of intimacy between God and us. Our second priority is to have an attitude of goodwill toward each other. We try to follow Philippians 2:3–4: 'Do nothing out of selfish ambition or vain conceit, but in humility consider others better than yourselves. Each of you should look not only to your own interests, but also to the interests of the others.'"

"As newly remarrieds, we worked to establish a godly marriage by going to a marriage retreat, attending a marriage conference, and being part of a remarried couples Bible study," Isabel and Marcos say. "And years later, we continue to date and learn about each other and how we can make our marriage strong. For our entire life, we intend to remain committed to continuing to grow in our marriage."

It's also wise to form healthy daily habits of showing affection, giving affirmation, choosing intimacy, and deepening your spiritual life together. Fill your marriage adventure with love, laughter, work, fun, romance, sacrifice, and forgiveness. Most of all, be patient with your mate—and your children—and trust God to mature each of you as you become more like

Him. He knows the plans He has for you, and they are plans to prosper your marriage and give you an amazing journey together (Jeremiah 29:11).

While you're on this lifelong adventure of remarriage, romance will give you the mountaintop experiences you crave, companionship will help you walk through the mundane fields and boring pathways of life, and

Ways to Strengthen Your Marriage

- **Be friendly.** Develop couple friends your age as well as older couple friends who can help you walk out the day-to-day life of marriage.
- **Be social.** Get involved in a Bible study together, and spend time with other second-marriage couples who can journey with you through life.
- **Be supported.** Find a mentor couple with whom you can be honest, open, and accountable to help you grow in your marriage, a couple who is a real-life example of a healthy marriage.
- **Be accountable.** Ask a same-gender friend to hold each of you accountable to holiness in your lives.
- **Be aware.** There are seasons in marriage when romance may wane or challenges may become overwhelming. Never give up on your marriage; work through any trials as a team until you come to a place of mature, unconditional, lifelong love.
- **Be a lifelong learner.** Read books, go to marriage-enrichment conferences and retreats, and keep on learning about your marriage and blending a family your entire life.

unconditional love and commitment will take you through the valleys that are less than enjoyable. When you encounter rainstorms or road-blocks, don't even think of abandoning the journey. Instead, repair the road and weather the storm. When one of you is tired and weary, hold the other up, encourage each other spiritually, and affirm each other in love. And when you're both struggling, find others to help.

"Be sure to find other second-marriage couples to help you navigate the journey," Megan and Tom suggest. "Find some role models who have walked where you're walking and can help you through. Don't try to do it alone."

Love through the Years

As the years go by and your marriage deepens and matures, be careful not to get apathetic about your relationship, and remember what a great adventure your second marriage has been and can still be. While it's easy to take each other for granted, it's important to reengage as soon as you realize that your relationship is beginning to slip. All that takes is a mini-date or a look at your photo albums or a walk in the park or a few extra deposits in your mate's love bank. That might mean getting her flowers, as Dale so often does, or making a favorite dessert for him, as I (Susan) do. It's surprising how little it takes for the return on investment. Never, ever stop investing in your relationship.

As with any journey, there are slow, boring, mundane seasons, but the times of making memories, capturing intimate experiences, and finding quality moments can supersede all the rest. Choose not to get discouraged or weary in working on your marriage, in resolving conflict, or in strug-gling to blend your family.

Like any couple, you may experience little frustrations again and again. We mentioned earlier that Dale and I (Susan) have learned to laugh at one of our minor frustrations—talking to each other from another room and sometimes from another floor, expecting the other person to hear and respond! While we could get frustrated with each other, we choose to laugh about it instead.

Build memories that transcend everyday life. It's a daily choice . . . to love unconditionally, to sacrifice substantially, and to enjoy each other as long as you both shall live.

"We both were so used to doing it all that we expected to continue to do it all on our own after we married," Linda and Rick say. "Not so! We suddenly found ourselves in a partnership of giving. It's just a wonderful thing to be married to someone who serves and loves you unconditionally!"

It's also good to remember that regular physical intimacy is crucial to a healthy marriage. Especially if you have children, there will be times you just need to get away, so plan to make regular time to do that. We try to take an anniversary trip every year, but if you have young children, you may need a monthly retreat, even if Grandma or a friend simply takes the children to her house for the night so you can get time alone in yours.

"The key to keeping your marriage strong is making sure everyone understands that your relationship comes first," Karen and Paul say. "Activities are great, but when you're out five nights a week and are too tired for intimacy or communication, then you risk having an unhappy marriage."

When your marriage is threatened by you, your spouse, your children, and others; or when your thoughts, actions, or attitudes draw your heart away from your relationship; or when temptations or the deceitfulness of your own heart tells you it's just too hard; or when work, kid stuff, or mere exhaustion turns you away from your journey together, fight for your marriage! At such a time, it's critical to regroup, get counseling if necessary, and return to the great adventure you've set out to accomplish together. Let God lead and guide your marriage and family life, and let Him inspire you, give you new dreams, and help you establish fresh goals.

Because Susan and I (Dale) know that health challenges will eventually take their toll, we've determined to do all we can now to make memories and enjoy our time together. Then, when we're housebound and can no longer enjoy the freedoms we now have, we'll look back and know that we've lived with no regrets.

Marriage is so much about walking out your faith on a daily basis. On this great adventure called marriage, as you join God in the plans He has for you, you can become more like Christ and learn how to reflect Him with your words and actions.

"It's important to speak often of God's blessing and His active hand in our lives," Tina and Karl say. "Living with a God-in-the-same-room attitude is so important. When we sense His nearness, it helps curb selfish comments or mean actions toward the other person. God wants our marriage to thrive, and He is always present, watching and waiting to help."

You can show the world how God can take two imperfect people and redeem their lives for His glory. And your second marriage in Christ can reflect that intimate and holy relationship of the Trinity.

Just the other day, my (Susan's) son reminded us how much our marriage speaks to our loved ones as well as others. He called just to chat, but he also talked about how glad he is that Dale is in my life, and he told Dale that he was glad Dale was in his life! Family and friends have expressed their gratitude that God brought us together, and we wholeheartedly agree. Through all the ups and downs, our marriage is a beautiful thing. Oh, what a great adventure awaits those who put God in the center of their marriage!

✿ BLENDING WITH KIDS

What about the Blending-Family Journey?

Even though preparing for a second marriage is complex, you've also seen that blending your family can be even more complicated. Here are a few final tips to help you on your way—from those who've been there and done that:

- Determine whether your kids are ready for a blending-family journey, and be open to patiently waiting for them to get on board.
- Keep your priorities straight and regroup when you need to.
- Be united in all you do.
- Create a culture of grace.
- Establish long-term family goals.
- Cut yourselves lots of slack!

Only you can assess whether your children are ready for the blending-family adventure. Younger children may adapt fairly easily, while older children may try to sabotage your relationship and the potential for a healthy blending family. Discern wisely.

"Talk a lot about each of your children's unique personality traits, and discuss how your future spouse might be able to relate best to each child," Isabel and Marcos suggest. "If you can, long before you marry have all the children meet each other and just have fun together. Talk to your own children about the idea of blending the two families together in marriage, and listen to their feelings and ideas. Then wait on your marriage plans if any of your children are adamantly against the changes that a marriage may bring."

"Always keep your family structure clear," Tina and Nick say. "It's one of the most important things you can do to keep your marriage in the right priority. It should be God first, then your marriage, and then your children after that. But that's a tough thing for kids to understand when they've been on center stage in your life and have never had to be dethroned by someone else. So have patience and treat them with the utmost sensitivity and care. But when push comes to shove, your spouse must come first! You definitely have to portray a united front in all you do. Even if the kids try to pull you apart, stay united. Even when you don't agree on something, be a team, and then later talk about it privately."

"From the start, make it clear to your kids that your marriage comes first and that you love this person and expect them to honor and respect your spouse too," Megan and Tom say. "Set this expectation early on so your kids can see your commitment to the remarriage adventure. Unless you do, the kids will likely manipulate the situation for their benefit. If you're strong about this, it'll draw your family together more quickly."

But keep in mind that your children are facing lots of change—they now have to share their parent with you. So be gentle, patient, and kind as you establish these new roles and family ties.

"Create an environment of grace, and live in it," Sharon and Zach say. "Giving grace means loving someone in spite of their flaws and the things that irritate you. That will breed trust and safety, and it will bring healing. And always be open to learning all you can about how to blend a family better. It isn't easy, so you need all the help you can get! Get counseling, read books, and do what you need to do."

"Take it a day at a time, and lower your expectations of blending your family," Tina and Nick say. "What you can expect, even require, is that every family member respect one another and treat each person with kindness. It may be rocky for several years, your stepkids may never really accept you, and the kids may never really feel like siblings. You have to be okay with that. How quickly your family blends will be different for every family, so let it be what it is."

"We've established long-term goals for our family, and that strengthens and unites our family," Hannah and Tim say. "We want to build a Christian worldview and work ethic in our kids, so we try to be a good example to them and model these things well. We also want to show our children that the world doesn't revolve around them, so we show them how to serve others, to experience the world, and to participate in the Great Commission."

Balancing a blending family can be a challenge, but it can also bring rewards beyond measure. Seize this incredible opportunity to see God's redemption reign in your life as a couple and in the lives of each of your children, and you'll experience a truly redemptive journey.

⚘ APPRAISING MY LIFE

Are you ready for this adventure called remarriage? Are you ready to weather the storms that may come your way? What storms might you anticipate? Can you commit to allowing the Lord to lead you in your marriage and your blending family?

⚘ ASSESSING OUR LIVES

Discuss the following questions together.
- How do you feel about blending your family?
- What do you need to do to further prepare for this unique journey?
- your marriage?
- for your blended family?

⚘ A MOMENT FOR FUN!

Take a few moments to talk about your wedding vows. Do you want to use traditional vows or write your own? What's the significance of making vows to each other?

What would be the best wedding gift you could receive? The worst?

❧ APPLYING GOD'S WORD

Here are a few Scripture verses to encourage you on the rest of your second-marriage journey:

> Therefore, I urge you, brothers, in view of God's mercy, to offer your bodies as living sacrifices, holy and pleasing to God—this is your spiritual act of worship. Do not conform any longer to the pattern of this world, but be transformed by the renewing of your mind. Then you will be able to test and approve what God's will is—his good, pleasing and perfect will.
>
> For by the grace given me I say to every one of you: Do not think of yourself more highly than you ought, but rather think of yourself with sober judgment, in accordance with the measure of faith God has given you. Just as each of us has one body with ... these members do not all have the same f ... are many form one body, and each membe ... We have different gifts, according to the grace gi ... be sincere. Hate what is evil; cling to what is good. Be devoted to one another in brotherly love. Honor one another above yourselves. (Romans 12:1–6, 9–10)

> "No eye has seen, no ear has heard, no mind has conceived what God has prepared for those who love him"—but God has revealed it to us by his Spirit. (1 Corinthians 2:9–10)

> We are God's workmanship, created in Christ Jesus to do good works, which God prepared in advance for us to do. (Ephesians 2:10)

Notes

Preface

1. Research cited in Jason Williams, "Talk Before Tying the Knot," *Psychology Today*, July 1, 2003, http://www.psychologytoday.com/articles/200308/talk-tying-the-knot.

Chapter 4

1. Adapted from Willard F. Harley Jr., *His Needs, Her Needs: Building an Affair-Proof Marriage* (Grand Rapids: Revell, 2001), 7–8, 35.

Chapter 5

1. Albert Mehrabian, *Silent Messages: Implicit Communication of Emotions and Attitudes* (Belmont, CA: Wadsworth, 1971).

Chapter 6

1. Ron L. Deal, *The Smart Stepfamily: Seven Steps to a Healthy Family* (Bloomington, MN: Bethany House, 2002), 148–51.

Chapter 8

1. Ben Woolsey and Matt Schulz, "Credit Card Statistics, Industry Facts, Debt Statistics," February 28, 2012, CreditCards.com, accessed March 20, 2012, http://www.creditcards.com/credit-card-news/credit-card-industry-facts-personal-debt-statistics-1276.php#Credit-card-debt.

2. Washington Asset Building Coalition (WABC), "Why Does Asset Building Matter?" accessed March 20, 2012, http://www .washingtonabc.org/node/122.

Chapter 12

1. Steven Curtis Chapman, "Echoes of Eden," *All About Love,* copyright © 2003, Sparrow Records.

Recommended Reading

Following are several books we suggest you read during your first few years of marriage. You will find them helpful in strengthening your marriage, and they will also help you succeed in the adventures of blending your family.

Deal, Ron L. *The Smart Stepfamily: Seven Steps to a Healthy Family*. Minneapolis: Bethany House, 2006. This book provides practical, realistic solutions to the issues stepfamilies face. The author also provides perspective and wisdom for the challenges of stepparenting and stepchildren relationships.

Deal, Ron L. *The Smart Stepdad: Steps to Help You Succeed*. Minneapolis: Bethany House, 2011. Designed specifically for men stepping into the role of stepfather, this book offers solid, easy-to-understand advice over a wide range of issues.

Alsdorf, Ray, and Debbie Alsdorf. *Beyond the Brady Bunch: Hope and Help for Blended Families*. Colorado Springs: David C. Cook, 2010. Blending a family is far more complicated than many of us realize. The authors' personal experiences of working through stepfamily life will help stretch hearts, minds, and homes past the image of "perfect" into the hope of God's promise to restore, heal, and build a blended family.

Deal, Ron L., and Laura Petherbridge. *The Smart Stepmom*. Minneapolis: Bethany House, 2009. A stepmom all too often gets classified as "the wicked stepmom" of the *Cinderella* story, but she doesn't need to be. This book is written specifically to the stepmom who wants to be a positive influence, fend off rejection, let her husband lead, and learn how to handle the challenges of blending a family well.

Smalley, Gary, and Greg Smalley. *The Heart of Remarriage*. Ventura, CA: Gospel Light, 2010. Not sure you're quite ready for remarriage? Dig deeper into healing the hurts of your past and learn how to create emotional security.

Deal, Ron L., and David Olson. *The Remarriage Checkup: Tools to Help Your Marriage Last a Lifetime*. Minneapolis: Bethany House, 2010. As couples work through this book in conjunction with an online Couple Checkup, they'll discover ways to improve all aspects of their marriage and build on its strengths.

Slattery, Juli. *No More Headaches: Enjoying Sex and Intimacy in Marriage*. Colorado Springs: Focus on the Family, 2009. Women, do you want to understand more about the intricate dynamics of sexual intimacy? This book is for you!

Harley Jr., Willard F. *His Needs, Her Needs: Building an Affair-Proof Marriage*. Grand Rapids: Revell, 2011. This classic book helps you discover the different priorities of men and women and offers insights into the intimate emotional needs of husbands and wives to strengthen your marriage.

Chapman, Gary D. *The Five Love Languages: The Secret to Love that Lasts*. Chicago: Northfield, 2010. What is your primary love language? In this classic book, Chapman shows you how to unselfishly show your spouse love by sharing it in the way he or she can best receive it.

Eggerichs, Emerson. *Love and Respect*. Nashville: Thomas Nelson, 2004. More than anything, a man needs respect and a woman needs to feel loved. When these core needs are met, each partner is happier and the marriage is healthier. Eggerichs helps couples learn how to communicate so they can meet the most important needs of their spouse.

Palmer, Scott, and Bethany Palmer. *First Comes Love, Then Comes Money: A Couple's Guide to Financial Communication*. New York:

HarperOne, 2009. Money conflicts are one of the primary reasons relationships end, but the authors teach you how to keep that from happening. This book provides you with financial communication skills that will show you how to talk about money and how to work together to build a solid financial future.

Clarke, David. *Kiss Me Like You Mean It: Solomon's Crazy in Love How-to Manual.* Grand Rapids: Revell, 2009. How can married couples overcome the obstacles that derail their desire and return to being "crazy in love"? Blending humor and practical advice, Clarke offers answers from the Song of Songs.

Peel, Kathy. *The Busy Couple's Guide to Sharing the Work and the Joy.* New York: Picket Fence Press, 2009. This book offers you the tools you need to divvy up your parenting and household duties and grow a stronger family as you develop teamwork techniques.

About the Authors

Susan and Dale Mathis are the authors of *Countdown for Couples: Preparing for the Adventure of Marriage*. As a happily remarried couple themselves, they are passionate about helping couples prepare for marriage and for remarriage. Susan and Dale have worked with a variety of couples in premarital counseling and have been mentors and facilitators for a megachurch premarital ministry, encouraging and equipping couples with vital and helpful information.

Dale has two Master's degrees in counseling and has worked in counseling and human resources for more than 30 years. He is a retired Air Force Lieutenant Colonel and specialized in personnel matters during his 20-plus years of military service.

Susan is the founding editor of *Thriving Family* magazine and the former editor/editorial director of 12 unique publications, including the *Focus on the Family* magazine and the *Focus on Your Child* newsletters. Susan was also a Christian schoolteacher for nine years and a missions' curriculum developer for the Association of Christian Schools International. She has written hundreds of articles and columns for magazines and newspapers and is the creator of smWordWorks, where she serves as a consultant, freelance editor and writer, and a speaker.

Susan and Dale enjoy traveling nationally and internationally and have visited more than 30 countries together. They also like to participate in the great Colorado outdoors by camping, hiking, and biking. Between them they have five adult children and three granddaughters.

To contact Susan and Dale visit their Web site: SusanGMathis.com or e-mail them at SusanGMathis@gmail.com.

FOCUS ON THE FAMILY®

Welcome to the Family

Whether you purchased this book, borrowed it, or received it as a gift, thanks for reading it! This is just one of many insightful, biblically based resources that Focus on the Family produces for people in all stages of life.

Focus is a global Christian ministry dedicated to helping families thrive as they celebrate and cultivate God's design for marriage and experience the adventure of parenthood. Our outreach exists to support individuals and families in the joys and challenges they face, and to equip and empower them to be the best they can be.

Through our many media outlets, we offer help and hope, promote moral values and share the life-changing message of Jesus Christ with people around the world.

Focus on the Family MAGAZINES

These faith-building, character-developing publications address the interests, issues, concerns, and challenges faced by every member of your family from preschool through the senior years.

For More INFORMATION

 ONLINE:
Log on to
FocusOnTheFamily.com
In Canada, log on to
FocusOnTheFamily.ca

 PHONE:
Call toll-free:
**800-A-FAMILY
(232-6459)**
In Canada, call toll-free:
800-661-9800

THRIVING FAMILY®	FOCUS ON	FOCUS ON	FOCUS ON
Marriage & Parenting	THE FAMILY	THE FAMILY	THE FAMILY
	CLUBHOUSE JR.®	CLUBHOUSE®	CITIZEN®
	Ages 4 to 8	Ages 8 to 12	U.S. news issues

Rev. 3/11

More expert resources
for marriage and parenting . . .

Do you want to be a better parent? Enjoy a stronger marriage? Focus on the Family's collection of inspiring, practical resources can help your family grow closer and stronger than ever before. Whichever format you might need—video, audio, book or e-book, we have something for you. Visit our online Family Store and discover how we can help your family thrive at **FocusOnTheFamily.com/resources**.